MW00464674

ZODIAC SPELLS

ALSO BY LEXA ROSÉAN

PowerSpells
Easy Enchantments
The Supermarket Sorceress's Enchanted Evenings
The Supermarket Sorceress's Sexy Hexes
The Supermarket Sorceress

ZⴲODIACSPELLS

Easy Enchantments
and Simple Spells
for Your Sun Sign

Lexa Roséan

St. Martin's Griffin 🐾 New York

For
Tracy Morgan

ZODIACSPELLS. Copyright © 2002 by Lexa Roséan. All rights reserved.
Printed in the United States of America. No part of this book may be used or
reproduced in any manner whatsoever without written permission except in the case
of brief quotations embodied in critical articles or reviews. For information,
address St. Martin's Press, 175 Fifth Avenue, New York, N.Y. 10010.

www.stmartins.com

Library of Congress Cataloging-in-Publication Data

Roséan, Lexa.
    Zodiacspells : easy enchantments and simple spells for your sun sign /
Lexa Roséan.—1st St. Martin's Griffin ed.

        p. cm.
    ISBN 0-312-28544-2
    I. Witchcraft. 2. Charms. 3. Astrology—Miscellanea. I. Title.

BF1566 .R645 2002
133.4'4—dc21

                                                                2002068354

First Edition: October 2002

10 9 8 7 6 5 4 3 2 1

C⊕N✝EN✝S

ACKNOWLEDGMENTS

I really need to thank:

"El Pulpo," for fixing my computer, sharing information about South American folklore, and most of all, cooking for me.

Juan Pablo, for sharing information about South American folklore and doing the dishes.

Raffaele, for the gnocchi, frutti di bosco, and panettone.

Adriana Groisman, for sharing information about Argentine politics and her husband Alberto's cooking.

My automatic writing partners:

Alina Troyano, for writing with me and cooking for me.

Madeleine Olnek, for writing with me and cooking for me on the fabulous Ronco Showtime Rotisserie Oven.

Shirley Kwan, for writing with me and cooking for me.

Carol McCurdy, for writing with me and cooking for me.

Broadway, Pywackett and Kishka, for being great company.

Nicki, Garbo 180, and the Goddess, for bringing me luck and inspiration.

iMac, for cooking with me.

Vivian and Alejandra, for their scary witch stories and cooking for me on the Ronco Showtime Rotisserie Oven.

Jennifer Enderlin, Sandra Martin, Lisa Hagen—even tho' you never cooked for me, you have taken me out for lunch and dinner. I deeply appreciate the opportunities you have given me.

FOREWORD

I was inspired to write *ZodiacSpells* by the need to create more personal recipes for individual practitioners. Often when spells don't work it is because the ingredients do not vibrate well with the person performing the spell. In an attempt to overcome that problem, I offer you personal astrological spells to tune into your individual needs for protection, health, money, success, and love. Each ingredient is chosen because it vibrates accurately to each sign's specific needs. Also included are chapters to help you enhance the strengths of your sign and to combat the weaknesses. I don't know about you but I often hate buying books on astrology. I feel like I'm paying for twelve parts and only one part applies to me. In Zodiac-Spells, each spell can potentially be used by *all* signs. I want you to get your money's worth and I hope indeed it all proves a good read!

For example, if you are an Aquarius there is a money spell for you. You may work this spell at any time of year. However, you might find it more lucrative to perform the Aries money spell in the springtime. This organic way of working allows you to tap into the energies that are in season. Experiment and see what produces the best results for you.

More advanced practitioners can layer even deeper. Suppose you are a Libra with 03 degree Aries ascendant. That would make Taurus cusp your second house of money. This is a very powerful position: a double prosperity whammy. Imagine your results when performing the Taurus money spell at any time of year, but especially when the sun is in Taurus which means it is transiting through your house of money. The spell should bring you threefold prosperity. On the other hand, using the Libra money spell (because your sun sign is Libra) might draw money to your business partner or spouse in the seventh house (but not directly to you). Get it?!

These spells can be worked on the simplest and on the most advanced levels. Don't worry if you don't know a lot about astrology or your individual chart. Start with your sun sign and work your way up as you learn more. The worst attribute in magic is doubt. Don't doubt yourself. Clear, confident, unconfused magic is the most effective. Do not try to move above your level or you will create doubt and the spell will not work. None of this should seem complicated. The information is very straightforward and those on a more advanced level will easily understand the layering process. If you don't get it, it means you are not ready for it. Trust me!

Your Zodiac success spell can be used for general success. It can also be used by anyone in a profession ruled by that sign. For example, if you are a writer you may use the Gemini success spell, regardless of your sun sign. If you are a Gemini, you may also use the Gemini success spell no matter what you do for a living. Here again, you can layer. Let's say you are a

Scorpio who practices law. Do the Scorpio spell for personal success and the Libra spell for success with your law practice. It's that simple.

The same principal applies to Zodiac Health. Each sign has a ritual to protect their overall health and well-being. But anyone having a specific health problem should use the spell of the sign ruling that illness or afflicted body part. I want you to get 100% out of *ZodiacSpells*.

A plethora of spell books are appearing on the shelves. This year I saw a spell book written by a Catholic nun. The popularity of magic, the oldest form of prayer, is growing. Many people have trouble connecting, and experience the eternal busy signal when trying to reach God. The Old Religion has much to teach in the ways of communicating with and calling forth the divine energy (God and Goddess). Spells are to be used to develop the spiritual muscle in conjunction with all the things you do to develop your other muscles in life. They are not shortcuts to fulfill our every capricious whim, but rather petitions to higher powers and symbols that unblock and strengthen our own will to succeed. Ritual does not have to be elaborate, but it must be approached with reverence and made special and sacred from the mundane. You can eat a tomato or YOU CAN EAT A TOMATO! My recipes are not meant to be mixed or prepared during the commercial break of your favorite TV show. They require your absolute attention and an attitude and atmosphere of reverence. Consider yourself a spiritual warrior when you perform a spell.

Remember the words of Hermes Trismegistis: "It is a wise man who rules the stars. It is a fool who lets the stars rule him." The zodiac is not God, but a creation of God, given to humanity to help us navigate and reach our destinations. From the sailor at sea to any man or woman who reads an astrology column, the stars have served as a guide. May these *ZodiacSpells* steer you successfully to your magical destination.

Blessed Be

Lexa Roséan

Zodiac Protection and Safety Spells

You can use magic and spells as a spiritual shielding system. Each sign has a built in mechanism of defense: its own aspect of protective energies. Each sign has herbs, spices, minerals, or other natural ingredients which reflect the protective nature of that sign. Using the strengths of each sign, you can work a protection spell for every month of the year—and the way things are going you may need one. Use these spells respectively all twelve months of the year to enhance your circle of security or use the spell for your sign year-round for extra added protection.

HEADS UP

watercress

The head is the most vulnerable part of an Aries and must be protected. The sign subjects one to dangers such as head injuries, brain overload, blind rages, paranoia and, of course, losing one's mind. Avoid injury to yourself and others by using this spell. Vincent van Gogh was an Aries who suffered from severe mental breakdowns throughout his life. During his most famous attack he cut off a piece of his own ear! Senator Eugene McCarthy was the kind of Ram whose thinking caused damage to others. He completely lost his rational head and began seeing RED around every corner. (Red, by the way, is the color of Aries.) Heads up, Aries!

Watercress is ruled by Mars. It greatly affects the brain and is said to sharpen and improve the wit. The Greeks and Romans ate watercress to sharpen their mental abilities and keep the head properly aligned. Eat watercress on Tuesdays to protect your head and balance your temperament. When used on a consistent basis, watercress can help produce clear and concise thinking during any crisis situation. Remember, though, ancient soldiers ate it to *prepare* for battle. They did not wait until the war was raging to stuff their mouths with the leafy greens. Aries will benefit greatly by adhering to the

Boy Scouts' motto: "Be Prepared." Other signs should prepare by working this spell on all Tuesdays while the sun moves through Aries (March 21–April 19).

SECURITY SPELL

INGREDIENTS

barley
bananas

Taurus magic should be used to protect the physical body, material things, and assets. Barley is sacred to earth and Venus, the ruler of Taurus. In ancient earth magic rituals barley was sprinkled around areas and goods to protect them. You can sprinkle barley around the four corners of your home or office to protect your belongings within the space. You can also carry barley in your pockets to protect your person. Bananas are sacred to this sign and can be eaten to protect the physical body during transit. Eat bananas on or before a journey (by car, boat, train, bus, plane, or foot) to protect yourself. The outer skin of the banana is symbolic of a shield that protects the more vulnerable and precious soft fruit within. It is customary to save the outer skin of the banana as a talisman to protect you on your journey. You may wrap the skin in a bag and place it somewhere close to you. Once you arrive safely at your destination, you may dispose of the peel. A rather nice ritual, if it is at all possible, is to place the peel next to a rose bush. The peel contains nutrients for these plants and the rose is sacred to Venus. In this way you can complete the ritual by giving something back to the earth and the goddess in gratitude for her protection.

The Taurus or Taurus ascendant may perform this spell as needed. The banana also works quite well for the traveling Sagittarius. Other signs will find most success when the sun is in the sign of Taurus (April 20–May 21).

FORESIGHT

INGREDIENTS

mace (the outer covering of the nutmeg)
marjoram

Hindsight may be 20/20 but mace and marjoram bring foresight. They create awareness and lend protection. Good sources of information can defend and protect against potential danger. Use this Gemini potion to invoke intelligence and open channels. It can be used for the good of the world or for a personal situation. For example, it could be used to uncover terrorist plots but you might also need it to find out what the lawyer of your about-to-be ex-spouse is up to. Or a former (or current) business partner. Information for protection can be used on many different levels. I have found this spice and herb in very well-stocked supermarkets and green markets. You may have to search a bit, but they are definitely available. Both are ruled by Mercury and are considered aggressively fast workers. Sprinkle them around or carry them when you are trying to uncover information. Inhale the scent of each to speed up your search. Leave some out in a bowl on a table while you are having a conversation with someone you are try-ing to obtain information from. Please know that when I say *mace* I am referring to powdered mace, which is the outer cas-ing of the nutmeg. It is a spice used for cooking. I am not referring to mace, the spray, which is used for an entirely dif-ferent type of protection.

The Gemini may use this spell at any time of the year. Other signs are advised to use (or at least prepare) when the sun is in Gemini (May 22–June 20).

TO PROTECT CHILDREN

INGREDIENTS

mashed potatoes
cauliflower

Cancer is the most protective sign. Its domain is the home and children. (For a spell to protect the home see the **Spe-cialty of the House** section). Cauliflower and potato are two of the most protective lunar foods. The effects of both are said to be long lasting because the potato is a root vegetable, and therefore its magic runs deep. The cauliflower flowers or blooms, and it is therefore believed to perpetuate energy. Feed these foods to your children to protect them from danger. They can also be eaten by adults to protect the inner child. When potatoes are mashed or whipped they are reduced to the most gentle and loving aspect of their nature. Mashed potatoes are also considered "comfort food" and can reduce stress and worry. All parents (regardless of sun sign) may use this technique at any time to protect their children, as parental protection always falls within the realm of Cancerian influence, but the spell is most potent when performed while the sun is in Cancer (June 21–July 20). If used once in the year with strong visualization, it should lend protection to your children year-round. You may still repeat when necessary while following practical real-world commonsense methods of safety and protection.

On the subject of protecting children, I must address the subject of children and witchcraft. Through the years I have received many letters and E-mails questioning my view on teenagers and witchcraft. I do not believe I have ever put these views into writing. Here goes . . . sorry kids, but this momma witch puts spells in the same category as drinkin', drivin', votin', and goin' to war. You should be over eighteen, in some states make that twenty-one, to partake. The sixteen-year-old can be given a sorceress apprentice permit and cast spells under adult supervision. Teens should not attend Wiccan study groups without written parental consent! The practice of magic can be dangerous for one who is not properly prepared. My friend Gloria has a very talented young daughter who is quite gifted in the psychic realm. While Gloria was ferociously protecting her daughter from drugs and young bucks, Miss Thang was messin' around with the magic. It took Gloria over a year to clean the house of spirits, goblins and ghosts, hosts of incubi and legions of demons. You name it—Miss Thang had conjured it up! Scary stuff. She will make quite the witch some day, after those teenage hormones calm down. Youth has a wonderful raw energy but it must be carefully disciplined before applied to the magical arts. To protect your children from witchcraft, place some rosemary in their shoes and in their bellies. Season their pizza with it on full moons.

Now let me play the devil's advocate. Don't be surprised if your children turn to witchcraft. Especially if watching DVDs with the remote while in the hot tub (or swimming pool) is the extent of the soulful experience you have provided for them. I see so many families that emphasize the material and neglect the spiritual. Children are perceptive. Children are hungry. Wicca is an earth religion and therefore close to the ground. Easy to grasp. It is playful and unpunishing. Attractive to hold. It is a loving metaphysical path and if the God and Goddess themselves could initiate your children directly, why then, you should be all for it. Unfortunately there are many unsavory characters out there cloaking themselves in Wicca. Children, and even adults, must be protected from these types. Secondly, there is a dark side to the path, an underbelly, and an abyss to cross safely before reaching enlightenment. A child born into this path will be properly prepared for this journey when it must be made. The critical concern regarding witchcraft is not over children born and raised in the ways of Wicca. The controversy arises over teens with no grounding who jump into the path. Imagine a teenage boy flirting with Judaism and being given a circumcision at thirteen years instead of eight days old. Or a teenage girl entering a Catholic church and receiving the host without ever having gone to confession. Or a young infidel being brought into Mecca. In these religions, foundations are laid early in life to prepare for the entering of sacred spaces or to accept the covenant of the faith. Spiritual cleansing takes place so that the benefit of divine energy can be received. In Wicca it is the same. So don't be so hard on the kids when they get into trouble with witchcraft. Obviously they are hungry for enlightenment and empowerment. Teach them how to protect themselves and be properly prepared. It is also not surprising that the child who is well grounded and educated in one of the patriarchal paths will wander into Wicca. This child is merely looking to discover his or her roots, for the Old Religion is the ancestor of them all. The ancient Hebrews trafficked with idolators and worshipped their gods. Unearth any church in Europe and you will find a sacred grove of the Goddess. Buried beneath the mosques and temples of the middle east lay the ancient Sumerian and Babylonian shrines. Discovering the roots of your religion can only ground you deeper into your chosen path.

THE WATCH

INGREDIENTS

carrot and ginger

The sharpening of the senses is what protects Leo. The Leo needs to be awake, watchful, quick and agile on the feet like the cat. The lion is more vulnerable at night and must develop the inner solar fire to protect him/herself. A keen sense of awareness and agility will keep this sign safe.

Carrot and ginger are fiery foods sacred to Leo. Carrots will sharpen the leonine eyes and ginger will quicken the pace. Drink carrot/ginger juice at sunrise or sunset for protection.

Visualize a golden globe of light emanating from your heart chakra.[1] See the orb of light growing until its circumference surrounds your whole body. Drinking at sunrise will protect during the day. Drinking at sunset will protect during the night.

Leos may use these ingredients throughout the year to invoke protection. Other signs should use them when the sun is in Leo (July 23–August 22). If you are not a Leo but find yourself in the spotlight and therefore vulnerable, you may also use at sunrise or sunset any time of year. This spell can also be used at any time if you are agressively hunting down criminals, on a manhunt, or keeping watch.

GERM WARFARE

INGREDIENTS

endive
salt
chicory

Unfortunately, these three ingredients will not protect you from bioterrorism. But of all the signs, Virgo would be the best to protect against such things. The neat freak rules the health of the physical body, the microscope, germs, and things not seen with the naked eye. Endive is eaten to

---

[1] The chakras are spiritual points (or wheels) of energy in the body. The fourth (or heart) chakra is located between the shoulder blades or in the center of the heart.

strengthen the immune system. Salt is used for purification and shielding. Chicory helps weed out the invisible. The combination of these three ingredients would serve as a Virgo talisman for detecting and avoiding germs and strengthening against them. Eat salted sliced endive and bathe in chicory herb for protection.

Virgos may use this method any time of year to clean up hazardous situations. All other signs should use this spell when the sun is in Virgo (August 22–September 21).

LEGAL PROTECTION

INGREDIENTS

rose

wintergreen

corn oil

Libra invokes the law for protection. It is the sign of the scales of justice. Libra magic can be used to enforce a restraining order, to obtain legal status in a country that makes you feel safe, or in any situation where your safety can be enhanced by a favorable legal decision. The Libran may take this bath at any time for overall protection. It will help to balance your karma and lead you toward good. Other signs should use only when necessary for this specific type of protection. The spell will be most effective when performed while the sun is in Libra (September 22–October 22). The spell may also be worked when the moon is in Libra. Check an ephemeris or astrological calendar to find these dates.

Rose, wintergreen, and corn are sacred to Venus, the ruler of Libra. Corn is closely linked with karmic matters, decision making, and judgments. Rose and wintergreen open the heart and promote helpfulness and cooperation. In combination these three are used to bring favorable decisions on crucial matters. Rose oil or water, wintergreen extract, and corn oil should be added to your bathwater. Soak in the tub for a minimum of ten minutes while focusing on the desired outcome. You may also carry dried rosebuds, dried wintergreen leaves, and dried corn kernels into the courtroom for protection.

KEEPING YOUR SECRETS SAFE

INGREDIENTS

dried scorpion or pimento

The best talisman of protection for the Scorpio is a dried scorpion. You will not find one in your local market. I often see them preserved as paperweights and sold in little five-and-dime stores alongside nature trails. I found large barrels of them in the airport gift shop in Salt Lake City, Utah. The talisman can be carried when you feel you are moving in extremely dangerous circles, or it can be placed upon an altar for general protection. Anyone in the spy or espionage trade is advised to obtain one of these talismans.

In a pinch you may substitute a pimento when your safety revolves around keeping or revealing secrets. Hold a pimento under the tongue while visualizing your desired goal. If it is a secret that needs to be kept, swallow the pimento at the end of your visualization. If it is a secret you want to uncover, spit out the pimento at the end of your visualization.

The Scorpio may use these techniques year round. Other signs may use only when the sun is in Scorpio (October 23–November 22).

TO GAIN THE SIGHT

INGREDIENTS

sage

maple sugar

Jupiter is the most protective planet and the ruler of Sagittarius. The specific protective attributes of Sagittarius are vision and foresight. Preventative protection magic is certainly a type that is needed in the twenty-first century. The ability to suss something out, see danger coming and thereby avoid or circumvent it, is priceless.

The maple and sage are both sacred to Jupiter. Native American myths about the maple claim the tree was a gift from the god Nanabozho. This complex deity is associated with the end of the world and is also attributed with the power to re-create the world. He is the leader of the Grand Medicine Society and it is thought he will return to the earth before the end of the world to re-create it. Using his talisman may help to prevent disastrous endings and help to re-create more positive outcomes. It is the desire of the collective unconscious to view disastrous atrocities repeatedly because the subconscious desires to change their outcomes. What consciously seems like morbid behavior is actually a subconscious attempt to heal and change. Sage is an herb of wisdom, healing, and change. It is also known as "ghost medicine" and can be used to chase away bad dreams, depression, and fatalistic thinking. The earliest manifestation of Sagittarius was the Babylonian war god, Nergal. The centaur is a visionary warrior and the guide of the zodiac. Think of him as the one who points out hidden mine shafts beneath your feet and guides you to the safer path.

To begin this spell you must visualize yourself as an archer who is preparing to take aim and is standing guard against danger. By performing this spell or carrying this talisman, you will notice a heightened sense of awareness and an ability to circumvent disaster and dangerous situations. Make a tea of sage and season with maple sugar. Drink for vision or add to bath water to uncover danger before it crosses your path. Carry dried sage leaves and hard maple sugar in your pocket when traveling to avoid danger and harm. All Sagittarians and Sagittarian ascendants may use this magic constantly. Others are advised to use during November 21–December 20.

ROCK OF PROTECTION

INGREDIENTS

a rock with a natural hole

The strongest protection spell for Capricorns involves the use of a natural talisman. You must find a rock or fossil with a hole in it. I have found many such talismans in rocky mountainous terrain or on the beach. Since the symbol for Capricorn is the goat with the fish tail, a talisman found in either a mountainous region or an ocean environment would serve as a fine protective amulet. The most powerful protective amulet would be the one found in a region or area which is mountainous with high cliffs that overlook the sea. A silk cord of black or red should be placed through the natural hole in the rock. Consecrate the talisman and then it can be worn around the neck. You can wear it at all times or keep it upon your altar and only carry it in times of extreme danger. The amulet can also be hung on the doorknob of the entrance to the house.

All Capricorns and Capricorn ascendants are advised to look for and prepare a talisman of this nature. Other signs are compelled to seek out such an item and hang it on their doors or about their necks during the sun's rulership of Capricorn (December 21–January 20).

NOTE: The item can be obtained at any time, but it should be consecrated during the Capricorn time of the year. A simple consecration would consist of:

1—Sprinkling the stone with sea salt.
2—Passing the stone through the smoke of an incense such as Frankincense; or even more powerful and effective, holding the stone up and having it blessed and consecrated by a strong north wind.
3—Dripping the wax of a white or blue candle upon the stone.
4—Dipping the stone in pure spring water.
Now it has been consecrated and blessed by the four elements.

PENTACLE OF PROTECTION

INGREDIENTS

star anise

Aquarian magic can be used to protect a group of people, individual freedom, an idea, ideology, or computer system. It can also be used for the protection of humanitarian or political rights. Aquarius is represented by the Star card in the tarot. This card holds great healing and protective energy. It represents the visionary. When a great and spiritual vision exists, it is hard to break through the energy field and harm that endeavor. The five-pointed star or pentagram is also the witches' symbol of protection. Star anise is sacred to Aquarius.

Place several whole star anise around an area you wish to protect. Put them in the four corners of a space you are planning to hold a large gathering in. You can also make a tea from star anise and drink for personal protection or sprinkle the waters around an area to be protected.

Aquarians may use the star anise throughout the year for general protection. Other signs may use while the sun is in Aquarius (January 20–February 19).

PSYCHIC SELF-DEFENSE

INGREDIENTS

fish

The most protective talisman associated with the sign of Pisces is the fish. It is the symbol of the sign itself and when eaten can provide spiritual protection from all danger. It is said that because fish live and breathe beneath the earth, submerged in water (the most protective element), they remain unseen or hidden from most dangers that threaten earthbound creatures. By eating fish, you can align yourself with their magical properties. A very potent spell is to carve your name and the name of your family members into the skin of a fish before you smoke, roast, bake, fry, or cook it. Your names will be heated into the body of the fish through the skin. This is said to increase your psychic ability for self-defense.

All Pisces and Piscean ascendants may eat fish at any time to increase their aura of protection. Other signs are advised to up their fish intake while the sun is in Pisces (February 19–March 20) for extra added protection.

ZODIACHEALTH

Astrology has been applied to the healing arts since the days of Hippocrates in 460 B.C. Ancient healers had knowledge of herbs sacred to each sign and were familiar with the parts of the body and their astrological assignments. Even in modern times, a good astrologer can predetermine that an illness is likely to occur by studying an individual chart. The birth chart reveals the body's secrets much the same way as genetic coding can be used to predict future health vulnerabilities. This is, however, a very advanced and individualistic method of working. This chapter deals with astrological healing in more general terms. In most cases I suggest the making of a talisman to create energy within the auric field. This is a gentler, less invasive form of magic than taking herbs internally. Each sign has its own healing herbs that correspond to specific illnesses. Many of these herbs are not easily obtained and you must work with a licensed herbalist to make sure you are taking what is right for you. There will, however, be some spells that require ingestion of ingredients. But these ingredients are easily obtained and are very gentle on the system. They will not harm you unless you have food allergies to that particular substance. Most of these spells involve creating a talisman for your individual sun sign. In some cases, the talisman for your sign may not be effective or may cause adverse effects. This can happen if your sun forms negative aspects to another planet. The only way to know this is by analysis of your individual birthchart by a trained astrologer. It is for this reason that I have designed the talismans to be as general as possible. They are as potent as is possible for a general heal-all to be. You may also use the talisman of any sign if you have problems with the part of the body associated with that sign. Anyone with serious health problems who wishes to explore this venue of healing on a deeper level should consult a professional herbalist/astrologer for one-on-one assistance.

WARNING: If you feel any adverse effects from these talismans, you should discontinue use immediately.

Aries rules the head and face. Cayenne pepper is said to protect the head. A talisman can be made using the principle of sympathetic magic. Obtain a head of purple cabbage. *Do not use your own head.* Place a piece of paper inside the cabbage head stating all problems that need to be healed. These ailments must be related to the head or face: allergies, acne, neuralgia, headaches, toothaches, gumboils or canker sores, burns or cuts on the face, smallpox, and fevers. Inflammatory diseases also fall under the rulership of Aries. The talisman can be made for these specific ailments, or as a preventative measure. Shake cayenne pepper powder over the head and keep as a talisman until the cabbage begins to wilt. As the vegetable deteriorates, imagine your problem losing power or strength.

Thank the talisman and dispose of properly. Repeat again as necessary. Aries may create this talisman to protect the head and face, for these are the most vulnerable areas of the sign. In this case, it is only necessary to perform the spell once a year, preferably within the month of your birthday. Other signs should create the talisman only if they are suffering from an ailment associated with Aries. In this case, the spell may be repeated as often as necessary until complete healing has been achieved.

Taurus rules the neck, throat, and voice. Diseases associated with Taurus are eating and drinking disorders, sore throat, abscesses, tonsillitis, gout, and bronchitis. Sage and thyme are the best healing herbs of Taurus. You may add them to the diet or stuff a red cloth bag with these herbs and rub it around the neck area to protect and fortify. Taureans may create the health bag on or around the birthday month and keep it for the whole year to invoke good health. Other signs should create this talisman to lend magical healing to neck or throat problems. In this case, I recommend wearing the bag of herbs around the neck as often as possible.

Gemini rules the arms, hands, and the nervous and respiratory systems. This sign also rules the thinking process. Since Gemini is an air sign, talismans that can be inhaled will work best on the system. Lavender is an herb associated with Gemini that can help to calm the mind and spirit. Oil of lavender can be placed on cotton balls and sniffed periodically to calm the nerves. You can also obtain a massage oil with lavender scent and massage it into the hands or arms for a calming effect. The dried or fresh herb can also be placed out in the open or on an altar for healing and calming vibrations. Gemini is ruled by Mercury, the planet of swiftness. Those born under this sign are easily stressed out from excess energy. The best remedy is a lavender bath to calm the fragile Gemini nerves. You can purchase a lavender-scented soap or add lavender oil or fresh lavender herb to the bath water. Geminis should work consistently with this herb to calm the nerves and maintain a healthy relaxed mental state. Other signs should use this remedy only for specific relief of Gemini ailments. Continue to work with lavender baths or scents until your condition subsides.

Cancer controls the stomach and breasts. Illnesses associated with the sign are asthma, cancerous growths, indigestion, ulcers, stomach cramps, and obesity. The following is a simple spell for healing Cancerian problems. Cancer rules the emotions and it is believed that illnesses associated with the sign arise from an excess of emotional baggage. This spell is designed to cleanse the aura and release any negative emotional energy that may be contributing to physical illness. Lettuce is sacred to the moon and the sign of Cancer. You must use a head of lettuce that is big and round and full like the moon. Lettuce is also a food of prosperity and well-being. The head of lettuce should be passed over and around the body from head to toe. You may need someone to assist you in this spell. If the ritual is being done as preventative magic, the lettuce should be moved around and down the body in a clockwise direction. This will invoke a magical shielding. If the ritual is being done to get rid of an ailment, the lettuce should be passed around and down the body in a counterclockwise direction. This will enable you to strip any negativity from your auric field. Cancerians tend to get pretty crabby and irritable when they are sick. This ritual can be done at any time over a sick Cancerian to lift their spirits and improve the healing time. If you were born with the sun in Cancer, you may do this whenever you are sick regardless of the nature of your ailment. Other signs should use this ritual along with other forms of healing when they are afflicted by diseases ruled by the sign of Cancer.

Leo is the sign of the heart and also governs circulation in the arteries. Convulsions, spasms, eye disorders, circulation problems, and jaundice are also ruled by the sign. Walnuts are one of the easiest foods to obtain for healing Leonine ailments. They can be carried whole and unshelled in the pocket to protect the heart. Walnuts can also be infused into the diet to strengthen and fortify Leonine vulnerabilities. The Leo can create a walnut talisman on or around a birthday to invoke good health all year long. Write your name in magic marker across the outer shell of a whole walnut. Surround the walnut with sunflower seeds to add longevity and keep on your altar until your next birthday. Other signs may make the talisman or eat walnuts (in addition to proper medical treatment) when suffering from problems of the heart or other Leonine illnesses.

Virgo governs the liver, solar plexus, and the intestines. All herbs, foods, or vitamins that cleanse and strengthen the liver and intestines should be taken by Virgos as these are the most vulnerable of their body parts. Endive is a healing food that Virgos respond to well. It is said to cool the liver and provides good roughage for the intestines. Magical lore associates endive with strengthening the body and enhancing sexual stamina. (So, what have you got to lose?!) Add endive to your diet as a magical talisman against liver or intestinal problems. If you are afflicted in these areas, use endive to meditate on a complete healing of these areas. Hold a whole endive between your palms and over your solar plexus. Visualize your liver or intestines being strengthened and healed. Maintain the pose and continue the meditation for at least ten minutes. Thank the endive when you are done. Do not eat this food as it may have absorbed some of the illness from your body. Thank it and dispose of properly.

Libra balances the kidneys. When not harmonized, illnesses such as kidney stones, inflammation of kidneys or bladder, lower back pain, body odor, flatulence, hallucinations, insanity, and/or skin problems can manifest. The best talismans to steady the Libran are kidney beans. They can be carried dry in the pockets or soaked and cooked and slowly infused into the diet. When carrying as a talisman, it is important to carry equal amounts of dried beans on both sides of the body. Kidney beans can also be used in meditation. Fill each palm with seven dried beans. Close your eyes and hold your hands out as if they were two scales. Visualize balance in your life and kidneys. The Libran may do this meditation whenever he/she feels out of whack to prevent physical weakness from occurring. Other signs should do the meditation only if they suffer from kidney problems or other Libra disorders. After the meditation, the beans can be carried (on both sides of the body) or placed upon an altar of healing. If placed on an altar, they should be arranged to form a circle. You may place a picture of yourself within this circle. The beans need only be replaced if they crack or get damaged in any way.

Scorpio controls the sexual and reproductive organs and all sexual diseases and reproductive afflictions. It is interesting to note that the first case of AIDS was documented when Pluto (the ruler of Scorpio) entered the sign of Scorpio. Pluto is the slowest-moving planet and takes 248 years to move through all the signs, unlike the sun's rotation, which takes one year. When Pluto moves through a sign it always brings drastic transformation. When dealing with the sign of Scorpio, the emphasis would be on death and sexuality as these are the main attributes of the sign. As of the year 2001, Pluto shifted into Sagittarius. The rockiest points always occur with the initial shift of a planet from one sign to another. Once centered in the new sign, Pluto will hopefully bring the world the benefits of transformation through spiritual and scientific enlightenment and space travel.

A very powerful talisman can be made with dried leeks to ward off sexual diseases and to guard and protect the reproductive system. **I NEED YOU TO ABSOLUTELY UNDERSTAND 100% THAT THIS TALISMAN IS TO BE USED IN CONJUNCTION WITH,** *NOT AS A SUBSTITUTE FOR,* **SAFER SEX PRACTICES!!!** Your name should be carved down the length of a fresh leek as if it were a totem. Then the leek should be hung upside down to dry. Once dry, it can be cut and carried in a small bag in a pants/skirt pocket below the waist and near the genitals. The leek is known for its healing properties and is believed to cleanse poisonous conditions and to ward off evil or danger. You can also infuse leeks into your regular diet for extra protection and good health. The Scorpio may create this talisman on or around their birthday and use it for one full year. Other signs should create the talisman in the Scorpio month (October 23–November 22) for optimum success and can continue to use it as a sexual healing talisman throughout the year.

Sagittarius governs the thighs and movement in general. Accidents that occur because of haste, during travel, or while exercising are associated with this sign. Blood pressure problems, rheumatism, goiters, and cancer of the liver and intestines are diseases associated with Jupiter and Sagittarius. Sage is the most powerful Jupiterian herb and is used for healing and purification. Since Sagittarius is a fire sign, it is best to burn sage and smudge the body with it. Light the dried herb and let it smoke like an incense. Pass the smoke over the whole body for purification and healing. A Sagittarian may carry whole dried sage leaves in a pocket for protection against injury through movement. Other signs may gather the whole leaves during the month of Sagittarius (November 22–December 21), place them in a pouch, and keep as a travel talisman for one full year. Any sign suffering from Sagittarian ailments may smudge with sage in addition to receiving proper medical treatment.

Capricorn owns the knees, bones, teeth, and skin. Arthritis, skin diseases, fractures, weak knees and teeth, rickets, leprosy, ruptures, corns, and warts are all associated with this sign. Wintergreen is a potent Capricorn herb of healing. It is most easily found as an oil or extract. To make a healing talisman for Capricorns or Capricorn illnesses, obtain a dried animal bone. The best animal is a goat but you may use the bone of any animal that walks on four legs. Save a bone from some meat you have eaten, such as lamb, beef, pork, venison, or goat. Let the bone dry out. Rub wintergreen oil or extract into the bone and place in a pouch or Ziploc bag. Carry this talisman or place upon an altar of healing. The talisman will be most effective when created during the Capricorn month (December 22–January 20).

Aquarius has authority over the calves, ankles, and bloodstream. Aquarian health problems include cramps in the calves, weak ankles, blood impurities, insomnia, epilepsy, hysteria, and paralysis. It can also affect one of the eyes since it is the opposite sign of Leo. Plantain leaves or its banana-like fruit can be used to combat the diseases of Aquarius. Eat plantains while the sun is in Aquarius (January 20–February 19) or create a talisman in that month to combat these illnesses year-round. Carve your name into a fresh plantain leaf and hang it out to dry in the kitchen. When the leaf is completely dry, fold it up or crumble it and place in a cloth or Ziploc bag and add to your healing altar. The fresh leaves can also be wrapped around the ankles for ten minutes to infuse healing energy into any Aquarian health problem.

Pisces rules the feet. Health problems include pain in the feet or toes, gout, enlarged feet, corns, bunions, and lameness. Seaweed is the most healing of the plants connected with Neptune and Pisces. Since Pisces is a water sign, it responds best to the element of water. Therefore, a magical bath containing salt water and seaweed is recommended to protect the health of a Pisces. The ocean is the best choice but a bathtub will do. Add three fistfuls of sea salt to the bathwater and fresh or powdered seaweed. Soak in the tub for a minimum of ten minutes. Pisceans can use this bath whenever they are not feeling well. Other signs may use it as a healing bath for a Pisces-related health issue. Seaweed can also be added to the diet to strengthen the Piscean constitution.

NOTE: If you suffer from any of the more serious diseases listed under each sign, you should investigate the path of herbal astrology further. As an alternative path to Western medicine, it has quite a good reputation. Many people use it in conjunction with traditional medicine. However, most of the herbs that you will need in the more advanced system of working WILL NOT be found at your local supermarket. You will have to visit a good herb shop with a licensed herbalist available to diagnose and direct you.

Z⊕DIAC♏⊕NEY Spells

This chapter contains twelve money spells. They may be used in the following ways:

1—You may use the money spell created for your sign at any time of the year.

2—You may use a money spell designed for another sign if you are in a profession traditionally ruled by that sign.

3—Regardless of your sign, you may want to try the money spell that corresponds to where the sun is at any given time of the year. This will enable you to tune into the energies operating in any given month.

4—On a more advanced level of working, you may choose to do the money spell for the sign that occupies or is transiting through the second house of your personal astrological chart. In order to work this way, you must have knowledge of your ascendant and the sign that rules your second house cusp.

MARSMONEY

INGREDIENTS

green tea

carrots

cinnamon

Aries is very good at initiating financial growth. This spell can be used by an Aires at any time because they will respond well to the prosperity ingredients aligned with their sun sign. Other signs looking to initiate new sources of income may use these ingredients when the sun is in the sign of Aries (March 21–April 19).

Green tea is sacred to Mars, ruler of Aries, and can be used as a magical aid to draw money. Water should be heated until it comes to a strong boil. Steep the tea in the boiling water and drink as hot as you can stand it. Mars responds very well to heat and it quickens the response to your request. It is very important to think about the money you want to acquire, or even speak your goals out loud, as you drink the tea. Continue to drink every Tuesday until your financial goal has been met.

Carrots increase vision and drive, and when mixed with cinnamon they become a money potion which also draws luck. The best method of preparation is to boil the carrots until they soften, then add cinnamon sticks to the pot to season. Honey may be added for more drawing power and flavor.

CASHCOW

INGREDIENTS

thyme
spinach

Taurus is the sign of financial security and occupies the second zodiac house of money. The key words for Taurus are 'I have.' Ruled by Venus, the sign appreciates luxury, and if any zodiac sign could produce magic to make the market bullish it would be Taurus. Thyme and spinach are both sacred to this sign.

Eat spinach seasoned with thyme on Fridays to increase your financial wealth. You may also make a talisman when the sun is in Taurus (April 20–May 20) using dried thyme and dried spinach leaves. Crush the two together, roll into a dollar bill, and tie with a green string. Carry this talisman in your purse or place within a stock portfolio. The earthiness of these ingredients makes them perfect magical tools, not only for money but for any form of material possession. Thyme is said to make investments (money) grow. Spinach gives strength and endurance and because spinach is also ruled by Jupiter it is associated with financial growth and expansion.

WEALTH SPRAY

INGREDIENTS

seltzer, sparkling water or champagne

The Gemini must attract the creative attentions of Mercury in order to draw money. Mercury can create opportunity and networking possibilities and he usually works at the speed of light. The ritual is very simple. Mercury and his spirits love all things bubbly and effervescent. Shake an unopened bottle of seltzer or sparking water and then open the bottle. Let the seltzer shoot and spray. This is an excellent way to open channels for making money. If you are looking to obtain larger sums of money I suggest you use a bottle of expensive champagne. Remember you have to invest to create return! After the effervescent liquid of your choice has sprayed the room about you it is important to drink some, along with leaving a glass as an offering for the deity. Place a piece of silver, or better yet a Mercury dime, into the offering glass to make it more pleasing to the quicksilver spirits. By spraying, you attract external opportunity. By drinking, you create internal drive to rise and meet the occasion. The Gemini is advised to use this spell on any Wednesday regardless of the moon phase. Other signs interested in sparkling up their financial connections can use the spell on any Wednesday when the sun is in Gemini (May 21–June 21) or during a waxing moon when the moon is in this sign.

MOONMONEY

INGREDIENTS

green cabbage

The sign of Cancer is ruled by the moon and Cancerians should pay great attention to the waxing and waning phases of the lunar orb. This sign will be more susceptible than all others to lunar influence and should never do money magic during waning moons (the period from the full moon to the new moon). So strong is the influence of the moon upon you, that you will end up diminishing your income as the light of the moon decreases! The best time for Cancerian money magic is on the full moons. Cook a whole green cabbage with a silver coin or eat with a silver spoon while visualizing prosperity. For a super shrewd money magic spell, begin on the new moon by cooking and eating brussels sprouts, and conclude on the full moon by cooking and eating green cabbage.

This combination will protect and increase your assets. This spell is truly designed for those with their sun in Cancer, but other signs may use it to draw money into the home or to draw prosperity for businesses such as real estate, contracting, construction, or home decorating. In such cases, the spell should be performed once a year on the full moon in Cancer[1] for best results.

---

[1]This will take place sometime in January when the sun is in Capricorn.

GO FOR THE GOLD

INGREDIENTS

saffron

alcohol

gold, bronze, or copper colored coins

Leos are ruled by the sun, and gold or bronze are the precious metals that belong to the lion. Fifth house money usually comes from gambling or stock market speculation. Leo money can also come from children or any other creative source. The best time to work Leonine money magic is in the morning with the rising sun. Begin this spell on a Sunday at sunrise.

Saffron is a highly prized and expensive spice cherished by the ancient world. It was alleged to heighten intuitiveness and joy, as well as increase wealth. Alcohol is ruled by Leo and is used to enhance and heighten pleasure (both spiritual and material). There is an old cooking trick that uses alcohol to quickly release the potency and rich color of saffron. Place a tablespoon of saffron in a mortar and add a teaspoon of brandy or any yellow-colored[2] alcohol. Grind with your pestle to bring up the attributes of the saffron. Mix this into a small bowl or dish filled with gold, bronze, or copper-colored coins. If the coins are really made of these metals, even better! Hold this dish of coins centered in both hands for several minutes each morning at sunrise and meditate upon your

---

[2]Goldschläger is great if you can obtain it, for it contains real bits of gold!

financial success. Leos may create this money bowl at any time of the year and use it constantly. If you feel the power of it is waning, you may recharge it by placing the bowl directly in the sun. You may also wash the coins in spring water and repeat the original procedure after one solar year. The money bowl is designed to bring happiness and a constant flow of cash into your life. Other signs looking to make money in the creative arts or other speculative ventures should begin the bowl on the first Sunday of the sun in Leo (July 23–August 22). Do the meditation every morning while the sun moves through the sign. On the last day place the bowl outside under the sun as an offering to complete the spell.

GNOCCHI MONEY SPELL

The following is a very effective money spell based on Italian/Argentine folklore. The spell belongs to Virgo but it may be performed by any sun sign during any month of the year. The spell is as follows: On the twenty-ninth day of the month, place some money under a plate of gnocchi. Eat the gnocchi on the plate, and after you are done lift the plate and put the money in your pocket, wallet, or purse. This gnocchi money is said to act as a talisman to draw more money into your pocket or purse. For practical (Virgo) reasons the spell is performed on the twenty-ninth day, it is close to the end of the month and is usually when people need money magic so they won't come up short in paying their bills. This is a form of folkloric peasant magic. Gnocchi is considered a cheap food so one is already saving money by eating inexpensive food toward the end of the month. It will be even cheaper if you cook the gnocchi at home.

The number twenty-nine is highly symbolic. There are twenty-eight days in the lunar cycle so the twenty-ninth day represents renewal or the new moon. There are thirty degrees in each astrological sign. The first degree is 00 and the last degree is 29. So twenty-nine represents culmination from an astrological standpoint and renewal from a lunar perspective. The twenty-ninth degree of every astrological sign is believed to hold potent magical power. Performing this spell on the twenty-ninth day of any month (regardless of the moon phase) brings extra potency to the spell. I suggest eating green or spinach gnocchi just to up the ante for money-drawing power. Gnocchi is a dough (representative of money), made with flour (cleansing), and potato (nurturing). Hiding money under a plate and then uncovering it symbolizes the revealing of hidden treasure or wealth. There is a long-standing magical tradition of placing ritually charged items into a wallet or pocket to create prosperity-drawing talismans.

Virgo is the sign of the service industry. This money spell is particularly prosperous for waitresses, waiters, and busboys as most people forget to remove their money from underneath the gnocchi plate!

NOTE: The Argentines have varying customs for the gnocchi spell. Some say you can only place a one dollar bill or note under the plate. Others say that you may use any denomination. They all agree it should be bills and not coins. My advice—if you are eating out, best to use a one dollar bill (instead of a hundred) just in case you forget to remove it.

Another custom is to fold a one dollar bill with a special fold so that the head of Washington (or any governing face) is divided in half: he has one eye on the past and one eye on the future. Keep this dollar in your wallet for good luck and recharge it on the twenty-ninth of every month. It is also customary to leave some gnocchi on the plate uneaten. This is done to insure you will always have a little something left over.

BALANCING THE BUDGET

INGREDIENTS

buckwheat

peas

Libra is ruled by Venus: the planet of love, peace, balance, and harmony. Libra professions typically include the legal system, public relations, prostitution, the visual arts, the performing arts, music, and all forms of partnerships. Green peas are sacred to Venus and are thought to draw peace of mind and prosperity. Peas can be eaten by Librans on Fridays to increase income in a way that will be pleasing to the senses. Buckwheat is also sacred to Libra and can be sprinkled around the kitchen to ward off poverty or added to bathwater to create more balance and harmony in the professional and financial world. Librans are quite fond of pleasure and luxury but will not work for the sake of money alone. The sign needs mental and spiritual stimulation in order to create motivation for the acquisition of material gain. The combination of these two ingredients creates a harmonious flow between the creative and the material paths. Peas create a pleasing environment and buckwheat can prevent overspending, which is another Libran problem. The scales often tip and Librans find themselves in financial trouble because of overspending. To balance the budget, place a bowl of dried peas and buckwheat flour in the home. Keep it out until you have squared things away financially. Librans may do this work at any time. Other signs in Libra-ruled professions may use these ingredients to draw money when the sun is in Libra (September 23–October 22).

STEALTH AND WEALTH

INGREDIENTS

black strap molasses
green jalapenos

Ah, Scorpio money—big corporate bucks, insider trading, taxes, insurance, fund-raising, alimony, money laundering, and inheritance. If you are grappling with any of these financial issues, you need to work with the energy of this sign. Scorpios can be both intuitive and sneaky about money. They love to spend it in a big way, especially if it belongs to someone else!

Black strap molasses has a very subtle nature and is perfectly aligned with Scorpio attributes. It can be used to attract and hold wealth in much the same way as a spider's web is used to trap flies. Green jalapenos can protect and guard financial secrets as well as draw financial gain. The combination of these two biting ingredients are the perfect Scorpio prosperity recipe. If you need to entice someone to reveal their financial secrets or stingtalk them into investing in you, I suggest you dab a bit of black strap molasses on your tongue and bite into a green jalapeno to give your words a magical edge. You can also place a dish of green jalapenos on a table and smother them in black strap molasses. This will act as a talisman to draw money into your place of business. If you have a specific goal in mind, leave the dish out until the goal is met. For long term goals, renew the dish every month on the new moon. Seeds from the green jalapeno may also be dried, anointed with a dab of black strap molasses, placed in a small bag, and carried in your pocket. Scorpios may use these recipes at any time. Other signs should only use them when the sun is in Scorpio (October 23–November 21).

GAMBLING LUCK

INGREDIENTS

maple sugar
peanuts

Sagittarians are very lucky and very generous with money. Archers do well with speculative ventures: gambling (especially on the horses), travel, and foreign investment. Maple sugar and peanuts are foods of prosperity, generosity, and luck. The peanuts should be roasted with maple syrup drizzled on top. When eaten they will align you with the best financial energy your sign has to offer. The peanut is actually a legume but its seed pods travel underground. Maple syrup originates from the sap of the maple tree. Therefore, both the peanut and the maple have grounding and rooting properties that are essential to Sagittarians, yet they are also connected with high and far-reaching goals. The combination of these Jupiterian-ruled foods will help you to hold on to your money without putting a damper on your adventurous financial spirit. A talisman can also be made from these ingredients and used for luck in gambling. Take an unshelled peanut and work a small hole into the shell. Using an eyedropper, insert maple syrup into the hole. The best way to achieve this is by melting the maple syrup down. Wrap the peanut in tinfoil and carry to the racetrack. Archers can utilize this magic throughout the year. Other signs involved in Sagittarius-ruled financial arenas should take advantage while the sun is in Sag (November 22–December 21).

OLD MONEY SPELL

INGREDIENTS

a potato
coins

The prestige- and status-seeking goat is actually quite conservative when it comes to money. Capricorns have strong business ethics, are very responsible, and use their resources wisely. Hating costly and unnecessary spending, the Capricorn knows how to save money and will invest with prudence and patience. This sign is willing to work hard for the money and will avoid get-rich-quick scams at all costs.

The potato is sacred to the moon, but when charred it metamorphoses itself and becomes sacred to Saturn. Because the root vegetable has such innate nurturing qualities, even after transformation it will only summon the most positive attributes of Saturn. In this case, prosperity through responsibility and wisdom. Take a potato and press ten coins into it. You may have to slit openings with a knife first to easily insert the coins. Roast the potato until its skin is charred and produces an ash. Let the potato cool and gather some of this ash. Open the potato and remove the coins. Rub them in the ash. Arrange the coins in a circle on your altar and place a brown candle in the center. Carve your name into the candle and anoint it with potato ash[3]. Burn the candle and focus on your long-term financial goals. The candle should not be burned all in one night, but rather ten minutes a day until it completes itself. In true Capricorn spirit, I expect you to diligently repeat this spell on a regular basis. Do not expect any overnight results. This is a serious spell for long-term financial gain and material well-being. Capricorns may make these brown potato ash candles throughout the year. Other signs looking to stabilize and save, or focus on long term financial success, should work the spell each day when the sun is in Capricorn (December 22–January 19).

---

[3]To properly anoint a candle begin at the center and rub up; return to the center and rub down.

WATERBEARER MONEY BATH

INGREDIENTS

turquoise
baking soda

Aquarius is an air sign but is also known as the waterbearer. This bath uses ingredients that open up prosperity channels for the Aquarian. All magical baths should be taken for a minimum of ten minutes. The practitioner should be relatively clean and should not soap down after the magical bath. You may shower or bathe with soap, shampoo (or whatever) beforehand if you wish. While in the bath, it is important to relax and open up to ideas about making money. When you leave the tub, wrap yourself in a towel or bathrobe and remain quiet for another ten minutes. Then you may go about your normal business of the day or night. Run the water at the temperature you desire and add three cups of baking soda or powder. Drop a piece of turquoise into the tub. Immerse yourself and soak. Have a glass or container handy as you will need to catch up water with the turquoise gem in it and pour it over your back and head. Repeat this eleven times. Please use a small specimen of the gem so that you do not knock yourself unconscious or injure yourself in any way. Baking soda and turquoise are ruled by Uranus and can be used to remove financial obstacles and inspire sudden insight into fortune and gain. Once you have taken this bath, you may carry the turquoise in your wallet or pocket as a money talisman.

The Aquarian may take this bath at any time. Other signs may use it when the sun is in Aquarius (January 20–February 18) to drum up business in the dead of winter.

STEP INTO MONEY

INGREDIENTS

seaweed
shoes
a coin
a fountain or pool of water

A very popular superstition claims that if you step in shit you will come into money. I do not know whether this is true or not. I have devised a special spell for Pisceans, who are ruled by the feet, to walk toward wealth. You won't have to get too dirty to do it either! Place a coin in your left shoe. Walk toward any open fountain or body of water. Take off your shoe and pick up the coin between your toes. Throw it into the pool of water and make a wish concerning your income. Ask Neptune to make this financial dream come true. Stare into the water with the big dreamy pools of your Piscean eyes. Put your shoe back on and tap the tops of both your shoes three times. Within twenty-four hours of making this wish, you must walk into an area where some form of seaweed is present. (I recommend a sushi bar.) Eat seaweed while tapping your feet beneath the table. Again focus on your wish. Prosperity will soon cross your path.

You can also take a footbath with fresh seaweed and twelve

coins. Soak your feet in this solution for twelve minutes. Play with, and pick up, the coins and seaweed between your toes. Dry your feet, put your shoes on, and walk to work, a job interview, or anywhere that you wish fortune to come your way.

Pisceans may perform this ritual at any time. Other signs, especially dancers looking for work or money, should do the ritual when the sun is in Pisces (February 19–March 20).

Z⊕DIACSUCCESS SPELLS

THE LEADER OF
THE ZODIAC PACK

INGREDIENTS

spring rainwater
fresh basil

Harry Houdini, Hugh Hefner, Spike Lee, Gloria Steinem and Thomas Jefferson were all founding parents and innovators in their fields. Aries are not just original thinkers but doers as well. Theirs is one of the most successful signs; however, capable of accomplishing much, or at least setting things in motion, they sometimes don't show up at the finish line. This spell is designed to add longevity and staying power to the Aries natural gift for success.

Spring rain holds a special magical power. It is sacred to

the sign of Aries because the spring equinox is marked by the sun moving into the sign of Aries. The spring rain nurtures and gives birth to all the spring flowers which make way for the summer blooms. The waters of spring set off a seasonal pattern of rejuvenation and push the earth forward toward the final harvest to complete the cycle. Gather a cupful of the first spring rain. Add it to your bathwater along with some fresh sprigs of basil. Basil is sacred to Mars and brings stamina and success. Basil was also a favorite of Roman soldiers and Aries is the sign of military leadership. General Patton was born under this sign. No matter what kind of warrior ram you are, this bath will summon success and help it to bloom and prosper. You must bathe for a minimum of ten minutes.

Aries may perform this spell at any time of the year (providing you have some spring rain on hand). Other signs may take the bath when the sun is in Aries (March 21–April 20) to summon leadership qualities.

BULL'S-EYE

INGREDIENTS

a game of darts

Taureans are very focused, grounded, and obstinate. These are their tools for success. After achieving success the earthy bulls stubbornly hang on to it. They are the guardians of Mother Earth. John Muir, the naturalist and environmentalist, was a Taurus and so was Mother Jones, who fought for the rights of

coal miners (the workers of the earth). Taureans like posses-
sions, including people or subjects, and their word is the law
of the land. They make solid rulers or politicians and are
strong but benevolent. Queen Elizabeth II, Eva Peron,
Catherine the Great, Maria Theresa of Austria, Golda Meir,
Madeline Albright, and Ho Chi Minh are all Bulls. But
Machiavelli and Hitler were also born under this sign. In
most cases they can be trusted with things, as they are guided
by Venus and love beauty, art, and good food. Shakespeare
was a Taurus and his words endure and continue to beautify
and enrich our lives.

A Taurus can be lazy so I have devised a spell to help you
activate your stubborn will and focus your way to the bull's-
eye of success. Write your goal or objective on a piece of
paper and tape it to the bull's-eye of a dart board. Strike it
with darts until you have hit the bull's-eye at least three times.
Then move farther back and try this again. Once you have
achieved three more hits, move farther back for a third time
to pierce your target. This spell will combat the shortsighted-
ness and inflexibility that Taureans sometimes have. Their
obstinacy prevents them from seeing the long-term vision of
their success. Good luck and may you hit your bull's-eye of
success.

SUCCESS SUCCESS

INGREDIENTS

cinnamon
orange candle
parsley
assorted beans

The Gemini spell for success should be performed on a Wednesday, the day of Mercury. Obtain an orange candle and carve your name into it. Rub the candle with cinnamon powder or pure cinnamon extract. The proper way to anoint a magic candle is to begin at the center and move upward toward the top of the candle. Begin at the center again and work your way down to the bottom of the candle. This method uses the principle of the hexagram or six-pointed star; two triangles interlocked, one pointing up indicating "as above," the other pointing down indicating "as below." The idea is to send your prayer up above and have it mirror and manifest on the earth below. Geminis respond well to the twin triangle principle, as well as all forms of mirror magic, because of the inherent duality of the sign.

Place your candle in a candleholder and surround it with a circle of assorted dry beans. Beans are ruled by Mercury and are the Gemini symbol of success. Let the candle burn until it is finished. You may put it out and relight it again but make sure that the candle completes itself at some point. Visualize your objective while staring into the candleflame. Make up a chant for success in your own words. Words are the most powerful magic of the Gemini. Cole Porter, Walt Whitman, Lillian Hellman, Dashiell Hammett and Spalding Gray certainly had a way with words! When the candle is completed, gather the beans and carry in your pocket as a talisman for success. Geminis can also bathe in parsley or drink parsley tea to quickly summon success.

Geminis can perform these spells any time. Other signs may perform these spells between May 21st and June 20th for success in communication, public relations, education or writing.

LUNAR LUCK

INGREDIENTS

steamed veggies with soy sauce

The process of steaming is ruled by the moon and the sign of Cancer. It is also a gentle way to open the path to success. You may use any vegetables that you prefer but they must be cut in rounds (like the moon) in order for them to draw positive energy for the Cancerian. The Crab is very shrewd but is not the luckiest sign of the zodiac. Leona Helmsley was born under this sign. Soy sauce should be used to season the vegetables as it is also ruled by the moon. Soy is considered a bean of good fortune and is associated with many Japanese household deities. The most successful place for a Cancerian is in the home. Prepare the dish in your home and visualize your success fully as you eat.

This ritual is best performed on Mondays throughout the

year for Cancerians. Other signs may use the spell for success in real estate or any issues concerning the home when the sun is in Cancer (June 21–July 20).

TAKE CENTERSTAGE

INGREDIENTS

pumpkin seeds
yellow candle

Leos always attract the spotlight whether they desire it or not. Jacqueline Kennedy Onassis is a perfect example of a Leo always standing in the sun. It's no wonder she always donned those big black sunglasses! Paparazzi scrambled to capture her image and bring every private moment to light. The whole world was obsessed with watching her. Marilyn Monroe was born a Gemini but she died a Leo (August 4) and her death propelled her image forever into the public consciousness. Fidel Castro is another Leo whose fame and rule have not diminished. Each year he remains constant as the rising sun, even after the fall of communism. The Leo can not help but take center stage!

Scattering pumpkin seeds around a yellow candle is the Leo spell for success. Pumpkin seeds[4] represent fertility and

---

[4]It is important not to eat any pumpkin seeds while you are performing this spell, for the seeds are considered to be the children of the goddess Oshun. Oshun is very Leonine and she does not respond well when her children are eaten up. So be prepared to remove all forms of pumpkin from the diet if you want success from this spell.

will help spread the word about you or reinforce your positive image. Yellow or gold is the color of the sun (Leo's ruling planet), and represents light and attention. Carve your name into the candle and surround with the seeds. When the candle finishes burning, gather the seeds and toss them outside into the grass on a sunny day. This magical action will help to center and spread your success.

Leos can perform this spell on any Sunday to increase their natural starlike qualities. Other signs pursuing careers in show business or needing to draw attention to themselves in order to achieve success should perform this ritual when the sun is in Leo (July 23–August 22).

VIRGINAL TACTICS

INGREDIENTS

bread
red wine or pomegranate juice

Virgos are practical and analytical in their approach to success. They are discriminating, modest, neat, always useful and love to be of service to others. The work of Margaret Sanger is one of the best examples of the highest vibration of Virgo fulfilled. An activist involved in public service and family planning, her ideas and way of thinking changed the world in a very physical way. This is the manifestation of Mercury ruling the earth sign of Virgo. The symbol for Virgo is the virgin. In ancient matriarchal times the word was used in a different context than that of modern times. A virgin was a woman who owned herself. She was not married or mastered by any man. Some of the sacred temple harlots were called maids or virgins and the word had no connection with the breaking of the hymen. It simply referred to a woman who controlled her own life and destiny. Sanger returned women to this old way of being. Her struggle to legalize birth control was the kindling that set the women's liberation movement ablaze. Sanger fought, and even went to prison, to give women control of their bodies and the freedom to choose how they lived their lives. Virgos are very successful in public service. They are not martyrs like Pisceans but they will dedicate their lives to giving to others. Mother Theresa was a Virgo.

This child of Mercury loves facts and details. They are very descriptive and prolific writers and communicators. Connected with the Hermit card of the Tarot, the Virgo is also a bit of a mystic and seer. No doubt, they are the perfectionists of the world. For the most perfect (and magical) example of Virgo literary genius I suggest you read Jorge Luis Borges! Virgos also make fine editors, educators, public health workers and, of course, psychoanalysts. Carl Jung was born with his natal sun in Leo. However, in the year he met Freud[5], and while he developed his concepts of the collective unconscious and the archetypes, Jung's sun had progressed into Virgo!

The magical talisman of success for Virgo is bread dipped in red wine (or pomegranate juice). In ancient times wine was produced by the sacred virgins in the Goddess's temples.

---

[5]Freud was born an obstinate Taurus, but it is interesting to note that his death occurred on September 23, 1939, while the sun was in Virgo!

After the patriarchal takeover this task was appropriated by monks. Pomegranates and bread are sacred foods of the earth goddess and this earth sign in particular. Virgos can eat bread dipped in red wine whenever success is needed. Other signs in Virgo-related professions are advised to eat this magical talisman when the sun is in Virgo (August 23–September 22).

SCALES OF SUCCESS

INGREDIENTS

autumn leaves of orange/red/gold with a bit of green

Aleister Crowley, the infamous occultist, was a Libra. He coined the phrase "Love is the Law"—which is as close to a Libra motto as you can get. Crowley's work covered both the light and dark sides of the scales and created a central reference point for modern occultism. Librans are concerned with balance, harmony, and beauty. Brigitte Bardot was a Libra, although having your sun in this sign does not promise physical perfection. It is usually those born with Libra ascendant that are guaranteed to have good looks! Nonetheless, most Librans can count on their charm and grace to bring success. This is the sign of the diplomat, artist and peacemaker. Eleanor Roosevelt, John Lennon, and Mahatma Gandhi were Librans. It is said that those born under this sign make the best lovers and lawyers. The city of Seville is a Libra—birthplace of Carmen and the legendary Don Juan! Johnnie Cochran Jr. was also born under this scaly sign.

To invoke beauty, art, and diplomacy with a touch of Libran grace, gather some fall leaves. The Autumn Equinox is marked by the sun entering Libra. This occurs on the twenty-first, twenty-second, or twenty-third of September, depending on the year. The autumn leaf with its beautiful spectrum of colors is the perfect talisman for Libran success. Gather them up and scatter on a table or altar. Place other symbols of the success you want to achieve in the center of your circle of leaves. You can cut pictures out of magazines to represent your goal or use some of your business cards, resumes, or job proposals. Even a product sample will work. The autumn leaf contains magical energy that brings about change and growth. The changing leaf captures the threshold and balance of the seasons and holds the aggressive element of air which is perfectly aligned with the Libran spirit. Fall leaves can also be ground into a powder and carried in a pouch in the pocket or purse as a success talisman.

Librans may store up leaves and use whenever necessary. Other signs in Libra-ruled professions will have best results when the sun is in Libra (September 23–October 22).

PHOENIX RISING

INGREDIENTS

allspice and ginger

Nastier than a speeding bullet . . .
More sting than a hornet's wing . . .
Able to sink to the lowest depths and rise up again . . .

Look! Up in the sky!
It's a phoenix!
Rising from the ashes!
It's Scorpio!

Here is the Superman sign of success. Not even kryptonite can stop a Scorpio, for like Rasputin, this sign is immune to poison. You will have to shoot and drown them to get rid of them. And even then . . . they will probably come back for their revenge! The mad monk was actually a triple Capricorn, (the other power-hungry sign) but he had Scorpio on the midheaven. According to some calculations, Rasputin also had Venus, the Moon, and Saturn in the sign of Scorpio. Ouch! This explains his rise from rags to riches and his power to mesmerize the Romanovs. Even after his death, Rasputin's curse fell upon the Royal Family and within two months they were murdered by the Bolsheviks. I'm warning you, don't ever try to cross a Scorpio in business. It is very bad luck. They are dangerous, vindictive, manipulative, and they know all your secrets. Even the ones you didn't know you had. They even command the respect of their enemies! Take the example of the Desert Fox: Rommel never drove that deep into Egypt. Furthermore, he could not keep the allies from landing in Normandy. The Germans lost the second world war. The General actually did die by poison; however, it was his choice. This Scorpio then rose to secure a successful place in history for his brilliant military tactics. You see, the Scorpio always bounces back! Masters of deceit and calculation, charismatic, psychic, and perceptive—these probers love to work under-cover (and under the covers!). My advice: "if you can't beat 'em—join 'em!"

Use allspice and ginger root to harness Scorpio energy. Then you, too, can swing your stinging tail and scare off the maddening crowd of competitors. Allspice and ginger are magnetic and trenchant, containing energies that recycle themselves. True to the Scorpio nature, they can assist the user in summoning superpower and success. The allspice and ginger root must be ground to a fine powder using a mortar and pestle. The mortar and pestle hold the secret key to Scorpio power. SEX! The mortar symbolizes the sacred womb or vagina and the pestle is the phallus. Bump and grind those ingredients till they bend over and fall like dust to your will. The true Scorpion must then gather this powder and rub vigorously up and down the tail. Other signs should rub a small bit across the coccyx, or tailbone, to summon success.

If you are a Scorpio, you may perform this ritual at any time of the year to strengthen your natural ability to rise and fall and rise again. Other signs must wait until the sun is in Scorpio (October 23–November 21). This spell is highly recommended for those in retail. Be invincible and ready for the holiday shopping spirit.

TAKE AIM

INGREDIENTS

assorted nuts

Thanksgiving is the earmark of the season of the Sag. The American holiday is always celebrated two or three days into the sign. It falls on a Thursday, which is the day of Jupiter, the ruling planet of Sagittarius. It's the time of year when things begin to move swiftly, just like the archer. My mind conjures up images of backwoods boys with beefy thighs aiming arrows at wild turkey. Earthy centaurs gathering nuts and cranberries in the woods for the great harvest meal. In tune with Sagittarius energy, people get on planes, trains and buses—traveling across the country for their holiday meals. And for those of us who, in the true Sagittarius spirit, have 'moved on' and away from our families and have no desire to travel home—well, we stay put and prepare a bird for the group of strangers that have now become our cherished friends. The month of Sagittarius brings true insight; gives us a peek behind the perfect Norman Rockwell scenes and shows us in a glaring light that they are just not so. We have not really made much progress at all. Instead of traveling far from home, we have merely managed through the years to gather together a group of intimates that closely (if not exactly) duplicates our original dysfunctional families. Ah, the spirit of Sag loves to tell it and show it like it is. . . .

My last holiday gathering I found myself cooking for two dear friends of the Sagittarius species. Of course, they both arrived hours late (another annoying symptom of this sign). They waxed philosophic about the significance of Thanksgiving as I silently fumed over having to wait so long to eat: Native Americans versus Pilgrims; freedom and giving thanks versus commercialism and the injustices done to indigenous peoples; the presidential pardoning of one turkey versus whether or not all birds should be pardoned; blah blah blah . . . On and on they went, searching for the true meaning behind the celebration.

"It's all about NUTS!" I finally put a word in.

"What are you talking about?" quizzed the Archerboy.

"What about the bird? Isn't it about the bird?!" demanded the Archergirl.

"It's not about the bird (although Donald Duck is a Sag). The secret, the true secret of the Thanksgiving meal is the nuts." I repeated, beginning the first magical lesson of the meal.

"Ah ha, I see. Well, nutty professor, please continue!" urged the Archergirl.

"*Chestnuts* in the stuffing. *Almonds* with green beans. *Walnuts* in the cranberry sauce. *Sunflower seeds* in the green salad. Sweet potatoes whipped with *hazelnuts*. And *pecan pie*. Not to mention the bread, with *sesame seeds* giving it that very nutty taste. Who brought the wonderful bread?" I asked.

"I did," smiled Archerboy.

"The red wine also has a very nutty, oaky taste," added Archergirl.

"I brought that, too," offered the boy.

"Well, I brought some pistachio nuts for later just because . . . well, because they were by the checkout counter in Balduccis," said Archergirl, not wanting to be outdone.

"That's nine nuts and Sagittarius is the ninth sign," I said wistfully.

"I think you're nuts about nuts because you don't have any!" sang out Archerboy.

"I just think she's plain old nuts," said Archergirl.

"It just so happens that the ancients ate nuts to cure insanity," I retorted, and continued on. "Thank you, Archerboy, for reminding me that I have no testicles. I do, however, have ovaries—the other set of powerballs. And hopefully each of us sitting at this table has a brain—for that is what the nut truly represents! Archerboy, you should be thankful for every girl who's nuts about nuts! However, the insinuation that nuts represent balls or testicles is a totally inaccurate analogy. Nuts more deservedly relate to the brain. And balls, try though they may to emulate the brain, are far beneath them."

"Now that's really hitting below the belt," sulked Archerboy.

"Furthermore, the nut is cased in a hard shell just like the brain. The testicles float in a thin little sack of skin," said I.

"Yeah, balls are really more like grapes!" laughed Archergirl.

"No, the egg is the food that regenerates itself. Balls are more like huevos and they have no place on the Thanksgiving table," I said, anxious to move on.

"No, no, some people in the heartland eat deviled eggs on Thanksgiving. As an appetizer—I'm quite sure of it," said the Archergirl authoritatively.

"Listen," I snapped, "eggs are for the springtime. NUTS are for NOW. Winter is coming and we need to squirrel things away. All these nuts sharpen the mind and give a philosophical bent to the spirit, which is important to heighten at this time of year."

"—A week before my birthday."

"—A day before mine," interrupted the two wisenheimers.

"Yes, happy birthday Archergirl and Archerboy," I continued. "You were born under the sign of wisdom, higher learning, philosophy, optimism, and religion. Eating nuts during this month will increase your potential for learning, for understanding the universe, and increase your spiritual knowledge or religious conviction."

"I'm an atheist," shouted Archerboy, while chomping on a walnut. "And I plan to remain one!"

"Yes, increase your religious convictions. Just as I said."

Archergirl was busy picking nuts out of all her food as I spoke.

"So, like, are nuts the secret key to my success, or what? Should I eat them all the time or just now?" she asked with her mouth full.

"The secret to success is to love what you do and do what you love," said Archerboy.

"Ah, spoken like a true Sag," said I and continued to answer her question. "The other signs can only benefit by eating nuts when the sun is in Sag (November 22–December 21). Sagittarians can infuse nuts into the diet throughout the year to enhance the innate wisdom of the sign."

Archerboy piped in, "I'm all for that. You girls should eat nuts all year. How about starting with mine?"

Did I mention that Sags have a very randy and lewd sense of humor? Archergirl began to protest. "Gawd, that's all you men can think about. One track mind. I'm trying to understand my own nature, advance forward, change and grow. I'm trying to learn something that can help me reshape and accommodate my adventurous spirit. I'm stuck in this miserable tight shell of my own existence and all you can think about is getting a blow job!"

Archergirl, who also has a Leo moon and Leo ascendant, then began to cry and dramatically threw her plate of carved bird and assorted nut-filled dishes across the room. It landed smack on a framed poster of Maria Callas (my favorite Sag) and broke the glass.

This mortified but ever-compassionate witch kept her cool and wistfully said, "Take energy from the nut to break out of the shell that constricts you. The nut will help you aim toward success on the mental, spiritual and physical planes."

I consoled Archergirl while Archerboy quickly cleaned up

the mess. We met in the kitchen, where I slipped some red pistachio nuts into his pants pocket. "These nuts love action, Archerboy. They should bring you lots of success in the egg department!" He smiled and parted with a quick kiss, anxious to check out the club scene. Archergirl stayed until the wee hours, following me from room to room pontificating upon the nature of life. I learned a lot that night and in true Sag fashion I have decided that next year I will make a change. I will travel back to my ancestral home and do Thanksgiving with my original nutty family!

GOATGODS

INGREDIENTS

gruyere cheese

The Capricorn likes to rule with an iron fist or behind an iron curtain for iron is the metal sacred to this sign. Reverend Sun Myung Moon, the cult leader of the "Moonies"; Joseph Stalin; and J. Edgar Hoover were all Capricorns. Talk about control freaks! Then there was Richard Nixon, Darth Vader, and Al Capone. Power-hungry with evil and criminal inclinations, the goat can be downright scary! Edgar Allan Poe and Rod Serling were Capricorns, too. It is one of the most successful signs, for Capricorns are driven and will stop at nothing to get ahead. On the upside, the goat has amazing bone structure, for Capricorn controls the skeletal system of the body. Marlene Dietrich was a fine example of the bony beauties this sign can produce. The symbol for Capricorn is a goat with a fish tail. This enigmatic endnote is often forgotten, but it lends a very mystical or puzzling side to the earthy practical goat. Nostradamus and the country of Afghanistan belong to this sign and illustrate this point. And, of course, there are the completely high types who have successfully integrated the goat with the fishtail: Martin Luther King, Elvis Presley (the King), and Jesus Christ (King of Kings). These types make the most lasting impression upon the world. They reach the pinnacle of material and spiritual success, for Capricorn rules the tenth house at the top of the chart. This is the highest place we can attain to.

If you are looking for more drive, more power, more status, and more rock-solid staying power this is what I suggest you do. First see a shrink and iron out some of your nasty pre-Oedipal and bitter Saturnian issues. Then take a big chunk of gruyere cheese (or something equivalent that is finely aged) and carve your name into it. Slowly consume this chunk of cheese over a ten-day period. As you eat the cheese, focus intently upon your goals for success. Aged cheese is sacred to Capricorn and represents a specific type of long-term nurturing that fosters incredible success and accomplishment.

Capricorns can perform this ritual at any time. Other signs looking for recognition should work this spell while the sun is in Capricorn (December 22–January 19).

PLUG INTO SUCCESS

INGREDIENTS
assorted electrical appliances

Tallulah Bankhead, Eva and Zsa Zsa Gabor, Edith Bunker, the Mad Hatter, Yoko Ono, Mother Goose, Ayn Rand, and the Loch Ness Monster. What a zany bunch of wackos! Those Aquarians are weird. Bizarre. Ruled by the unruly nonconformist Uranus—they are eccentric, unpredictable, and revolutionary. James Dean was an Aquarius but these rebels usually HAVE a cause! Uranus rules electricity and, of course, Thomas Edison was born under this sign. Aquarians always have bright ideas. It's the "light bulb going on above the head" sign. Aquarius is the genius of the zodiac. Key words are "I know." Mozart was an Aquarian. And Galileo. They are unusual, innovative and very political. Gertrude Stein and Bertolt Brecht were waterbearers creating new sounds. Above all—Aquarians are humanitarians and lovers of freedom! Abraham Lincoln could not have been born under any other sign. Their success comes from their ability to work within the group energy. They are highly evolved scientifically and creatively and not afraid to take risks. Often their eccentricity lends them charm and success.

This is the spell and it really works. Forget the candles and the incense. Turn on all the lights in the house. Turn on every single electrical appliance, as well. The vacuum cleaner, electric drill, the blender, coffee machine, humidifier, air conditioner, electric mixer, toaster, CD player, computer, radio, all the TVs and DVDs. All things that humm and whirl are especially powerful. Got it all going? Now shout out what kind of success you need. Uranus is present and listening! Shout your requests eleven times and then release the energy by throwing your hands up in the air. Bend down and grab your ankles to ground the energy. Slowly wind down and turn off all the juice. This ritual works very well with a group of people that have a common goal. Aquarians and groups of people may perform this ritual whenever success is needed. Other signs working solo must perform it while the sun is in Aquarius (January 20–February 18) to invoke originality and brainstorming.

FISH OUTTA WATER

INGREDIENTS

cloves

maple sugar

Pisces is not really a very successful sign even though they know it all. They've been there! They've done that! Well, I mean, there was Levi Strauss. He was pretty successful (although some say his success was jeanetic). And Albert Einstein. Yep, another relatively successful Pisces guy. But there is also Ted Kennedy. Lotta suffering there. Chelsea Clinton, Liz

Taylor, and Patty Hearst. They've gone through their share of hell. Pisceans are vulnerable and sweet and this is their best tool for success. No one wants to take advantage of a Pisces. In fact, of all the zodiac, this is the sign people are most likely to give their money to. No one knows quite why. It is just so. I imagine it is due to Neptune and Jupiter being their rulers. Jupiter is quite generous and Neptune, well, Neptune prevents you from thinking clearly.

Yes, these little angelfish provoke compassion and caretaking in all who encounter them. It's a dreamlike spell they weave over the other signs. They do it amazingly well as they have been around longer than the rest of us. They are ancient souls and shouldn't have to work that hard for a living. The eleven others must support them in their old age. They need to dream and live extravagantly to make up for all their suffering. All a Pisces need do is flap the fins and suck hard through the mouth like a fish on dry land struggling to breathe. Some Dudley DoRight will come dashing along to pay the rent and clean the fishtank. The Pisces will always prosper because no one can stand to see them in so much pain.

Here is a recipe to reinforce your irresistible helpless charm. Steep cloves in maple sugar and heat using the double boiler method. Remove from stove and strain. Let cool and then place a dab of the seasoned sugar under the tongue. Hold there for three minutes. Then roll the tongue around the lips three times clockwise. Both ingredients are sacred to Pisces and hold successful vibrations. Clove is used to invoke the benevolence of Jupiter. The prickly points of the clove also serve as reminders of suffering and pain. Maple sugar will reinforce your sweet demeanor and also draw favors and rewards.

This spell can be used at any time by a Pisces. Other signs should work the magic while the sun is in Pisces (February 19–March 20). I also recommend it for lazy and/or anguished artists looking for large federal grants.

ZODIACLOVE SPELLS

If you are reading this chapter, you already know that relationships are the most difficult part of life. Here are some magical remedies to give you a spiritual edge in the mysterious world of love.

ZODIAC LOVE ATTRACTION

INGREDIENTS

scented rose water
vanilla bean or pure extract
sweet almond oil or pure extract
dried lemon peel or pure extract

This is a general love recipe which can be added to the bathwater or worn as a perfume to attract a lover. The ingre-

dients should be mixed together in a bottle or jar and allowed
to steep for at least 24 hours for the essences to be released. It
is possible to make this recipe very specific by adding one
extra ingredient. The following is a list of love ingredients
sacred to each sign. Prepare the standard potion and add the
fifth ingredient for the sun sign of the lover you would like to
attract. You can also wear your own sign to make yourself
more appealing.

Aries—cinnamon stick
Taurus—red apple seed
Gemini—celery seed
Cancer—watermelon seed
Leo—dried orange peel
Virgo—pomegranate seed
Libra—cardamom seed
Scorpio—peppermint leaf or extract
Sagittarius—clove
Capricorn—dried cranberry
Aquarius—caraway seeds
Pisces—nutmeg

SOME LIKE IT HOT

INGREDIENTS

honey
red pepper
cinnamon
cayenne
carrot seed
cumin

Aries is known as the selfish sign in love. This is not necessarily a negative. To know how to please yourself is the first step in teaching another to please you. Also, if we can not appreciate and take care of loving ourselves, how can we be expected to learn how to love and appreciate another? Aries also loves to initiate. It is the sign that opens with the Spring Equinox, a time generally associated with the budding of new love. Aries has the least baggage of all the signs. Its drawback is that the sign sometimes lacks staying power and has a short attention span. Here is a spell to add longevity to Aries love and relationships. Use this spell to keep it hot!

Form a paste using honey and red pepper powder. Red pepper is ruled by Mars and Aries finds the spice very stimulating. It is used to instigate action and feeling. The honey will help to make those actions and feelings stick. This paste can be spread over a piece of paper with the name of a certain sun-in-Aries person written on it. Place enough of the mixture on the paper so that you blot out the name that you have written. In occult theory, the hidden factor is used to generate more magical power. Place the paper in a place where it is sure to absorb sunlight to add extra staying power. If you are an Aries, you can perform this spell on yourself to make you more constant in love. You can also perform this spell at the start of the spring to invoke a hot love affair that will last. In this case, use your own name. You may also work this spell on an Aries whose interest in you seems to be fading. Don't wait until the interest has already faded, for then it will be too late for this spell. Once an Aries moves on, that's it! Try to capture the spirit of interest and fire it up while it still burns hot. Imagine adding wood to burning coals. Within minutes, you will have flames. If you wait until the coals turn to cold ash, it does not matter how much kindling you add, because the fire has already gone out. The Aries needs to be fired up while still hot and then regulated to burn constant. You can repeat this spell as needed.

Aries also loves the chase; allow him or her to play this game. Sprinkle a mixture of witch's hunt powder in a path where the Aries is sure to walk to get them to make the first move. Hunt powder is made by grinding cinnamon and cayenne and carrot seed to a fine powder. Cinnamon draws; combined with cayenne it summons interest and action. Carrot seed promotes feelings of desire. "Some like it hot" would be the motto for most Aries. They are, by nature, fiery, impatient, and restless. But remember the Ram is also a little lamb. They can be gentle and loving and can follow as well as lead. A bit of cumin crushed between the fingertips can be rubbed between the eyebrows of an Aries to keep them happy, calm and faithful.

THE BULL OF VENUS

INGREDIENTS

red apples
apricots
cardamom
guava
strawberries
tomatoes
vanilla
apple cider
thyme

Taurus is under the rulership and possession of Venus. However, the constellation connects with the Greek myth of Europa, who had her eye on Zeus. He disguised himself as a bull, and when she climbed upon his back he took her off to his childhood home in the Dictean cave, and there they made love and she bore him children. The first step in seducing a Taurus is to get into the Bull's pit—den, digs, apartment, cave, or pad. They feel most comfortable when they have all their things around them. Peel an apple (sacred to Venus) and carve your name into the inner skin of the peel. Then core the apple and carve the name of the Taurus into the core. Wrap the piece of skin with your name etched into it around the core of the apple. Hold between your palms and chant:

Venus Aphrodite, Goddess of Love,
let me fly wrapped in the wings of a dove
into the home of———and the heart as well.
Influence———to the power of my spell.

Place this on your love altar as a talisman to influence the Taurus to invite you home. A love altar can be constructed simply by placing the four elements upon a table. Use dried seeds (apple or orange) for the element of Earth. Use an incense of love, a floral air freshener, or dried fragrant pot-pourri for the element of Air. Use a pink or red candle for the element of Fire. Use a bowl of honey-drizzled spring water for the element of Water. Any symbols of love or romance can also be placed upon this altar.[6]

If you are a Taurus, eat foods of love to invoke or keep a true love. Apples, apricots, cardamom, guava, strawberries, tomatoes, and vanilla are all sacred to your sign and to Venus in her most loving and sensual aspect. Eat these or work them into your diet on Fridays, for this is the most powerful day of Venus.

Possessiveness is the most negative attribute of Taurus: love is not something one can own. The heart of another person must be given and no amount of witchcraft can summon that—except for what is known as Gonzo or Zombi magic. This magic was practiced by Cagliostro. He used his charismatic powers to rob a woman of her will in order to have her love. Rent the movie *Black Magic* with Orson Welles for further

---

[6]For more on Love Altars see *The Supermarket Sorceress's Sexy Hexes* (St. Martin's Press).

details. If you find yourself obsessing and wanting to control another's heart against his or her will, I advise you to view this film and ask yourself again if this is the kind of love you truly want. I then advise you to bathe in a mixture of apple cider and thyme. Both are sacred to Taurus and are used for cleansing the heart, revealing courage, truth, and purification in love.

DOUBLE YOUR PLEASURE

INGREDIENTS

sweet almond oil or pure extract
mint oil or pure extract
pomegranate juice
Asian pear
various types of beans
celery
red pistachio nuts

There is no doubt that the Gemini makes the most interesting and intelligent lover of all the zodiac. They are full of fun and surprises and creativity. They give equal amounts of head and heart. The twins are the true communicators of the Zodiac: they need to feel you out mentally before they feel you up physically. You have to get into a Gemini's brain before you can get into a Gemini's pants or skirt. You must also be able to constantly and continually stimulate that large cerebral organ in order to truly get under the skin or into the heart of your Gemini lover. Sound like a lot of work? Well that's the drawback when you fall for twins. Double the work but double the pleasure.

To make yourself more interesting to the Dioscuri, bathe in fragrant oils of sweet almond and mint (the pure extracts will also suffice). Drink pomegranate juice to pull them in deeper, as the dualistic duo are famous for skimming the surface and then moving on. They are not really fickle, as people believe, but most often you bore them so they have to move on. Eat Asian pears and pink, red, and speckled beans on Wednesdays to improve your conversational skills and wit. They find versatility very attractive and it will help to keep their interest. The twins are an air sign and are very sensitive to smells. Scents draw the attention of the Mercurial ones outward, away from their busy cerebral worlds of thoughts and dreams and toward interaction with others. The way to a Cancer's heart may be through the stomach, but look to hook the Gemini by the nose! Bad breath or body odor are definite deal-breakers for this sign. The sweeter you smell, the longer they stay. One spring a white butterfly (totem of the Gemini) appeared in my garden and hovered over my prized yellow Iris. The flower was just about to bloom. Although there were many other fragrant varieties in the garden, this butterfly returned every day for two moon cycles to visit the same yellow iris. He touched no other flower. After a time, the iris bloomed full and died. One late afternoon as the sun was setting I noticed the wings of the white butterfly stuck to the dried iris petals. These soulmates left together to journey to the next world. Who says the Gemini can't be true?!

If you are a Gemini, I recommend adding celery and red pistachio nuts to your diet to bring creative fulfillment in love.

Your biggest drawback is that you may outgrow your partners. The seeds of the celery plant can also be carried near the heart to keep you satisfied and draw all the diversity that you desire.

All other signs may perform these spells during the Gemini month (May 21–June 20) to stimulate a more creative love life.

LUNAR LOVE

INGREDIENTS

melon

Melon is sacred to the moon and the sea. The fruit represents emotional, spiritual, and sexual fulfillment. Melons were used in the love rituals of many different cultures. Gypsy lore claims that the melon can help you obtain and keep your heart's desire. Cancer rules the fourth house of home and family. A stable relationship is most important to this sign; the crab wants to settle down and nest. Crabs can get pretty kinky but not until they know for sure to whom your heart belongs. They want fidelity and they want marriage. The white picket fence, complete modern kitchen, 2.5 kids with a live-in housekeeper will probably clinch the deal.

If you want to attract and hold the attentions of a Cancerian, bathe in the juice of a melon on Mondays or on the full moon. The Cancerian should hold a whole melon in both hands over the heart while meditating on the complete picture of love that is desired. Once the visualization is complete, the melon should be opened and eaten. This ritual should be done on Mondays or full moons and continued until the goals in love have been met.

MATING RITES

INGREDIENTS

red wine

It is impossible to write a love spell for Leo without mentioning fertility. Leo rules the fifth house of the astrological chart, which defines our sex lives and holds information about our children.

Here is a fertility rite from Bolivia: Huayra Tata is a very powerful god who rules the winds and hurricanes. He lives in mountain summits, deep caves, and abysses. He never shows himself except when he wants to make love to his wife Pachamama. Pachamama is the mare of the wind and mother earth goddess. Huayra Tata comes out and pours all his great waters upon Pachamama to make her fertile. Then he goes back into hiding and the waters of the earth become tranquil. The birthday of Pachamama is August first. She is a Leo. On this day there are very elaborate rituals done to honor her. Offerings of cocaine, alcohol, cigars, yicta and chicha are consumed and placed before her image. You will not find all these things in your local supermarket. However there is a very simple and beautiful ritual to Pachamama that is observed in Argentina. A glass of red wine is poured and the liquid is allowed to run over the glass and fall down upon the earth to mirror the seminal waters of Huayra Tata inseminating Pachamama. When a couple wants to conceive a child, the man should pour a glass of red wine and let it overflow onto the earth. The woman should take a small sip of this wine, and then the man must pour the rest of the wine onto the belly of the woman. The wine must roll off her belly and run down between her legs. This ritual should be done on August first and the couple should copulate immediately afterwards. If conception is being attempted with clinical assistance, the couple has until the sun leaves Leo (August 22) to fertilize the egg.

It is also customary to thank Pachamama after she has blessed you with a child. On the following August first, fill a clay pot with some food you have cooked yourself. It is best to make your own favorite dish or something you know you prepare well. Dig a hole in the ground and bury this pot as an offering of thanks to Pachamama.

For the Leo who does not want to conceive, but rather wants to increase sexual endurance, pleasure, length and number of orgasms—the ritual should be done as follows: The man must over pour the wine into a cup that the woman holds between her breasts. The wine should be allowed to run down her belly and in between her legs. The man must then kneel and lick every drop of wine from the body of the woman. The woman must then take some wine in her mouth and creatively anoint many of the man's erogenous zones. The couple is encouraged to continue pursuing their pleasure from there. They should continue with this rite until the cup has been emptied. Once the cup is emptied, the spirit of Huayra Tata and Pachamama will possess the couple and a hurricane of passion will ensue. These wind spirits love to get caught up in human form and they take full god/dess-like advantage and know all the secrets of pleasure to work upon the flesh. It is whispered on the wind that as long as no wine spills upon the earth, conception will not occur. **However,** Huayra Tata, Pachamama and I all recommend that you **practice safe sex** as you perform this rite. Both of these rituals may be performed by same-sex couples as well. The god and goddess of the wind do not discriminate based on sexual preference!

NO NUNSENSE

INGREDIENTS

dill

parsley

Ah, Virgo, you have discriminating taste. I envy you. So particular are you that you are probably alone! Or with a partner that you love to criticize and find fault with! Well, there is an up side to being picky. You won't end up with just any old admirer. You'll hang in there until someone comes along who really strikes your fancy, meets your standards, and is worthy of your love! Brava for you!

Here is a potion to draw all the exacting details you require in a mate. Parsley opens channels. Dill narrows them down. Dill is also a very powerful aphrodisiac. The combination of these two Mercurial ingredients can act like a sieve to sift out the undesirables and hold the desired catch. A bath should be drawn and sprigs of fresh parsley and dill added to the water. Visualize or list your criteria for a mate as you soak. With weekly use, you should begin to notice more of your detailed requirements being met. A partner you have already chosen and committed to may also be dropped in this bathwater to refine his or her behavior more to your liking.

Other signs may use this bath when more discrimination is required in choosing a lover.

SOULMATE SPELL

INGREDIENTS

cream of tomato soup with rice

Looking for a soulmate? Life partner? Libra love magic is the spell for you. Libra rules the seventh house of marriage and partnership. The sign teaches us how to have balanced nurturing relationships. Tomato is called the love apple and it is sacred to Venus, the ruler of Libra. Soup is ruled by the Moon. Tomato soup can be eaten (or bathed in) to flesh and round out a love relationship to its full potential. If you want magic to manifest an intimate and loving relationship leading toward commitment (or to secure and protect an existing commitment) add rice to your tomato soup. Rice is a grain with sacred magical/ritual connections to marriage and soulmates. Cream helps to nurture love and therefore allows it to grow. Usually creamed soup is connected with the nurturing love of a mother but tomato adds a kind of sexual twist. Add a dash of pepper to spice things up. Otherwise you will invoke too much maternal love.

This soup can be eaten on any Friday by Librans. Other signs should eat it on Fridays when the sun is in Libra (September 23–October 22). Visualize the kind of relationship or soulmate you desire as you eat.

SCORPIO LOVE BITES

INGREDIENTS

chile

mint

chocolate

Scorpio is the sign of sex. Ruled by Pluto, Scorpio also carries the vibration of obsession. To cause another to be bitten and smitten; to completely obsess over you, use this spell. Obtain a chocolate heart. The darker and richer the chocolate, the more effective the spell. Chocolate is ruled by Mars. Mars was assigned the original rulership over Scorpio before the discovery of Pluto. Chocolate is a food of love and craving. Carve the initials of the one you are after into the chocolate heart. Surround this heart with a circle of red, dried, hot chili peppers. Chile is sacred to both Mars and Pluto and is used for commanding and compelling. Obtain a fresh mint leaf. Mint is sacred to Pluto and carries the vibration of lust and obsession. Cut your initials into the leaf with a small knife. Or you may anoint the leaf with your saliva (by licking it) or you may anoint the leaf with a more special (private) bodily fluid. Lay the leaf on top of the chocolate heart. Chant:

By the depth of Pluto and the power of Mars,
from the heart of my beloved I remove all bars.
I command that he (or she)
obsess over me.
As I do will
so mote it be.

As you chant you must crush the red chili peppers one by one with a pestle. Then you must pierce and pound the heart with the pestle. Gather up all pieces and place them in a mortar. Continue to grind and mix the chocolate, mint and chile peppers. Keep repeating the chant as you empty the contents of the mortar into a double boiler, and begin to add heat so that the chocolate will melt. Allow the potion to cool slightly and then rub it on a red candle that you have carved both your names into. Light this candle and let it burn completely. Visualize your desire's heart burning and yearning for you. If at all possible, you may also feed your victim a Scorpio love bite. Obtain another chocolate heart and rub with red chili pepper and fresh mint leaf before serving.

SCORPIO LOVE STINGS

INGREDIENTS

horseradish
molasses

The **Scorpio Love Sting** is used for revenge—to get back at a lover who has jilted you. The spell is very nasty and utilizes the lowest form of Scorpio energy. There are three animal totems that symbolize Scorpio energy: The first is the eagle, which represents the spiritual heights that Scorpios can attain. The second is the serpent, which represents the rebirthing aspect of the sign. The third and unfortunately most recognizable, is the scorpion, representing the lowest, most poisonous depths of the sign. It is this element that will be utilized to work the spell. Before we begin I must note (and this is not a judgment—it is merely an observation) that anyone seriously considering working this spell is probably already deeply aligned with the lower form of Scorpio energy. It is quite possible that your nasty stinging attributes were the main cause of your lover leaving you in the first place. I suggest you take a moment for self-reflection and contemplate elevating your spirit to the serpent or eagle level. It might be wise to skip this spell and focus on self-healing, self-enlightenment, and/or moving on. However, if you insist on remaining in the depths, on lowering yourself to the level of petty revenge—well then—so be it. This is how you must proceed.

The horseradish is ruled by both Pluto and Mars. It is a bitter, bitter herb and is used in Jewish ritual (notably in the Pesach Seder) to symbolize the bitterness of slavery. Although in some households there is a humorous tradition of pointing to one's spouse to illustrate the bitterness of the *maror* (horseradish). To invoke a bittersweet revenge, obtain a whole horseradish on the full moon. One must use a whole horseradish for this spell. You can not use bottled horseradish. Be advised that this herb is not available year-round. It is most easily found in the spring. Using a sharp knife, deeply carve the name of your ex down the length of the horseradish. Cover the horseradish with a generous amount of molasses. Molasses is a true Scorpionic substance, in one of the sign's darkest, most sinister expressions and forms. The use of molasses will ensure that the bitterness you wish to inflict will have long-lasting sticking effects. If you are truly the vindictive Scorpio I think you are, you will Fed Ex this disgusting talisman to your ex. If you are (as I dearly hope) an evolved Scorpio, you will bury this talisman in the ground, thereby releasing your bitter vindictive feelings. This final procedure will liberate you from your pain and allow you to gracefully move on.

LA SELVA

INGREDIENTS

clove
black truffle oil

La selva is the jungle and dwelling place of the Sagittarian in love. Archers are adventurous in romance and like to explore unknown territory. They laugh like hyenas and do the dirty like hairy centaurs ravaging the forest or apemen swinging from vines. They are wild and uncouth; not at all refined. Are you still interested? Well then, here's how to land a Sag. Chew on cloves and rub drops of black truffle oil on your inner thighs. The Sag will pursue you like a wild boar on a magic mushroom hunt.

Sagittarians should obtain a red candle and carve the name of a potential mate or the qualities they wish for in a lover onto the surface. Anoint the candle with black truffle oil and pierce with cloves. Light the candle and let burn to completion. Visualize catching your prey.

THE BRINGER OF BAD LUCK

INGREDIENTS

thistles

cactus

white vinegar

In the 1930s and '40s, there was a very famous pianist, composer, and orchestra leader of Argentine tango. He was known as El Mufa (The Bringer of Bad Luck) or El Innombrable (The Unnamable). El Mufa is much like the "Scottish play." It brings bad luck to even say his name out loud. So superstitious are some of the people in Buenos Aires that even to this day, they will not play his music or mention his name in a milonga.[7] The Unnamable was also known as "El Tuerto" or "One Eye." The story goes that El Tuerto was desperately in love with a woman who shunned him. He tried to commit suicide and failed. Instead he put out one of his eyes. This was considered malo suerte. Very bad luck. Needless to say El Tuerto was a Capricorn. He also had Venus and Saturn in the sign. Capricorns are ruled by Saturn, the planet of bad luck and misfortune, bitterness and suffering. Actually, as far as I can tell, bitterness and suffering have their rightful place

---

[7]A gathering where Argentine tango is danced.

in the arena of love. So do not despair, dear Capricorns, there may be hope for you yet. The orchestrations of El Mufa are actually among the most beautiful of the tango compositions. Those who do not listen to them are missing out on one of the wonders of life. Interestingly enough, one of the last tangos that he composed and recorded was called El Abrojo/ The Thistle. Thistles are sacred to Saturn and are used in magic to drive away evil and bad luck. Thistles are also alleged to make men better lovers. If you cannot find a thistle, you can substitute a cactus.[8] If you cannot find a cactus, you can substitute pure white distilled vinegar. If you are using vinegar, you must anoint the corners of the eyes and have a good cry. Crying true tears over a thistle or cactus will also remove your bad luck in love.

THE COLD FISH

INGREDIENTS

chestnuts

The Aquarian is an emotional arctic zone, but I understand they are pretty sizzling in the sack. These zany robotic weirdos keep their feelings in the deep freeze but I've heard when they open up it's divine. You are going to need a roaring fire and a bushel and a peck of chestnuts to thaw this frozen heart.

---

[8]Please don't E-mail me asking where to find cactus. I have seen them on mountain tops, in the desert, and at florists, drugstores and supermarkets, too.

Chestnuts hold the magical vibration of love. They should be boiled for ten minutes and then each one slit with a paring knife. Place on a skillet over a roaring fire or in the oven to broil. They are ready for ritual once the shells pop wide open. Serve to an Aquarian you want more commitment and feeling from. Or eat some yourself to attract a new waterbearer.

The Aquarian can eat or carry chestnuts to attract a more permanent lover. (Other signs don't like to stay with you for too long.) Or being the freedom-lover that you are, you might opt for the filbert. The filbert draws partners for noncommittal sex, which might suit you just fine.

THE GLAMORFISH

INGREDIENTS

three large garlic cloves
three parsley sprigs
salt
tomato (peeled)
black olives (pitted)
one cup of sliced mushrooms
one tablespoon olive oil
½ teaspoon paprika
two pounds red snapper, whiting, or sea bass
  (cleaned and filleted)
fresh ground pepper
two to three cups water (enough to cover fish)
saffron rice

Pound garlic, parsley, and three pinches of salt together in a mortar and pestle. Work in peeled tomato and grind to a paste. Sauté paste in heavy pan with olive oil for three minutes. Add paprika and fish. Stir, and add water to cover. Bring to a boil. Add salt and pepper to taste. Boil for five minutes. Reduce heat and add mushroom slices and black olives. Simmer for ten minutes. Serve over cooked saffron rice.

Fish are ruled by Pisces, and among many other attributes, fish represent mystery and depth of beauty and character.

Paprika is a spice of love. Tomato is known as the "love apple." Garlic is an aphrodisiac and parsley opens channels and promotes lust. Salt, pepper and olive oil in combination clarify and accentuate your positive attributes. Mushrooms add glamour. Saffron brings wealth. Olives and rice summon true and long-lasting love. Yellow rice adds solar energy to put you in the spotlight. Eat this spicy fish stew to increase your glamour and sex appeal.

7 DEADLY SINS + 5

This chapter deals with the weaknesses of the signs. Each sign contains negative qualities. Just like a good pot of coffee gets concentrated toward the bottom and produces bitterness, or dregs, the tail end of each astrological sign also has its dregs. It is said that the later degrees carry the dregs. So, if you are born in the last degrees of a sign, you may tend to have more of that sign's negative qualities. Also, the last three days before the sun moves into the next sign tend to bring up the negativity or excesses of the sign as well. Consequently, everyone may experience the imbalance from three to five days before the sun shifts into the next astrological sign. Here are some ways to ritually combat the weaknesses of the signs.

THE WRATHFUL RAM

INGREDIENTS

fennel

Wrath, or anger, is one of the seven deadly sins and is definitely the downfall of Aries. Aries can be impatient and hotheaded when the sign is badly aspected. The positive qualities of strength, leadership and a head-first approach can reverse themselves and create temper tantrums and bursts of uncontrollable anger. It is important to remember that the Ram can also be the lamb and is capable of incredible kindness. Fennel cools off the heat and reveals the gentle aspects of Aries. Fennel also protects against and purifies anger. A fennel tea can be brewed and allowed to cool. It should then be used as a head wash to cool the passions.

Fennel can also be eaten on Tuesdays, the day of Mars, to strengthen the warrior. Mars is the ruler of Aries, and there is no escaping his martial inclinations. Yet, the spiritual warrior operates with compassion and foresight—not blind rage.

THE GLUTTON

INGREDIENTS

licorice root

The deadly sin of gluttony plagues the Taurus. The Taureans want to have it all, and because they are ruled by the luxuriant Venus their pursuit of pleasure can be excessive. Gluttony applies not only to food but to an exorbitant appetite for goods and people as well. Here is a spell to curb that "nothing is ever enough" feeling. Licorice root can be chewed to temper corporeal desire. One of the underlying causes of gluttonous behavior is the inability to receive things and take them in. This creates the obsessive drive to repeat and repeat intake while struggling to satiate the senses. Licorice is one of the most spiritual yin roots and teaches us to open up, accept, digest, and take things in. The Venusian ruled stem is also an appetite suppressant, plus it calms and subdues the spirit, helping to create a natural balance and limit the intake of pleasures. The natural root can be chewed on at any time to help combat the weakness of the Bull.

NERVOUS NELLIES

INGREDIENTS

lavender
fresh lemon
cinnamon

"There is nothing either good or bad, but thinking makes it so." Hamlet's words echo the downfall of the fragile Gemini mind. Too much negative thinking can devastate these nervous twins. The Mercury-ruled air sign must be careful of living life too much in the head. Worry, paranoia, anxiety, depression and nervous tension are all results of Gemini overthinking. Here is a magical potion to clear the air of too much thought.

Lavender is sacred to the sign and can help to alleviate overwrought mental conditions. A lavender scented air freshener can be sprayed about the room to calm down the mind. This is also an excellent remedy for all signs to use during the Mercury retrograde periods. During these backward motions of the planet, miscommunications abound. Lavender will help to clear up muddled thought, clarify communication, and greatly reduce stress levels during this planet's absence. During severe cases of mental distress, the Gemini should make a hot steam with fresh lavender herb. Place the lavender in a pot and heat up the water to just below the boiling point. Remove the pot from the stove. Place your face over the pot and cover your head with a towel. Let the scent enter your head to steam away excess thoughts and relax the brain. The steam should be followed up with a cooling ritual to make sure the mind stays clear. Cut open a lemon that has been cooled in the refrigerator. Cut in slices and place on the back of the neck and temples to cleanse the mind. Sometimes the Gemini has trouble focusing. Too many ideas or thoughts get in the way of accomplishing one simple thing. To remedy this, the twin should inhale the scent of cinnamon. The hot and fiery herb is sacred to Mercury and the Sun and will help you to quickly zoom in and center solely on your task. Do not use cinnamon unless you know what it is you need to focus on. Otherwise, you will provoke even more thoughts and aggravate and overload your already taxed-to-the-max brain!

THE PACK RAT

INGREDIENTS

cucumber
salt

The Moonchild is notorious for being a pack rat. They love to collect things and they have trouble throwing things away. Two years ago I helped a Cancerian move. Usually moving is a great time to get rid of stuff. Most people take this opportunity to prune down their belongings and let go of the past. Not this Cancerian. Boxes of papers from kindergarten through high school were loaded into the truck. Postcards from—and snapshots of—all her ex-lovers (even the ones she now hated!). Catalogs from defunct companies, broken furniture, the list goes on. It was most revolting when she actually packed up her cat box with two weeks' worth of dirty litter in it. I offered to help by emptying the box and adding fresh litter. Nope. She was insistent. She did not want to leave ANYTHING behind. Not even the dust!!

Here is a simple spell to help combat the weakness of your sign. The combination of cucumber and salt is very cleansing and can help you to let go. Cucumber is ruled by Cancer because of its watery nature. Yet the cucumber is also simple, direct and clean. Very zen. It can be used to create more order, less clutter in your life. Add salt for purification. Cut cucumbers into rounds and salt. Eat before cleaning or packing. You can also inhale the scent of cucumber to help you keep your home uncluttered.

Keeping in mind that you are a pack rat by nature, it is very likely that you also tend to misplace things around the home. Here is a spell to help locate lost objects in the home. It can actually be used by any sun sign at any time, because Cancer rules the home. This spell was given to me by an Argentine friend. He swears by it and so do I. There are many spirits of folklore who can be called upon for specific types of help. La CoMadre (the godmother) is a spirit who helps find things around the home.[9] You must call her name out loud along with the item you have misplaced and she will help you locate it. For example: "CoMadre please help me find my keys," or "CoMadre, I've lost my children can you help me find them?" CoMadre is known as the helper of mothers and households. She is definitely a spirit of the constellation Cancer.

---

[9]Note: For items lost outside of the home, see "Spell to Find Lost Objects" in my last book *PowerSpells* (St. Martins Press 2001).

THE LOFTY LION

almond
vanilla
chamomile
basil

Pride is the downfall and deadly sin of the Leo. Humility is the cure. The following is an old recipe to banish vanity and conceit. It is used to strengthen the spirit and center the soul. Haughty and showoff behavior usually arises from imbalance, insecurity and self doubt. The result is the "compare and despair" syndrome which then produces the "I'm better than everyone else and I can prove it" attitude.

Basil repels evil and strengthens the inner spirit. Chamomile quiets the need to prove our worth. Vanilla gives true self-esteem and almond summons awareness, intuition and appreciation of others. The combination of these elements creates a more humble soul. Use this potion to get rid of pretentious and arrogant behavior. Mix chamomile tea and basil leaves (dried or fresh) with drops of pure vanilla and almond extract. Leave this bowl out in a room to change the energies of those within the space. This is a great mixture to put out at board meetings or parties or any place where boring boastful people put a damper on everyone else having a good time. I personally find this mixture especially useful at gatherings where opera singers are present. These Leonine divas are usually impossible to endure without the fourth wall securely in place. Yet, once the lofty Lions get a whiff of my humble pie potion, they turn into meek purring pussycats!

THE NITPICK AND THE GOSSIP

INGREDIENTS

mud
salt
rye

Virgo's coveted sense of discrimination and refinement becomes a nightmare of nitpicking when this sign goes awry. Critical to a fault and pointing out every one of yours in microscopic detail, the Virgo is a disaster in its detrimental aspect. Their acute analytical ability reduces itself to an unprecedented anal-retentive royal pain in the ass. No one wants to be around a Virgo when they fall out of line and embrace the awful weakness of their sign. Everything possible must be done to spoil and soil the intolerable pristine qualities of the Virgin. We must smut, smut, smut them up. Break them in, dirty them up, and relieve them of these awful attributes! Salt, rye and mud muster the spirit and love of earthiness and allow the Virgo to let go, loosen up, live and let live, and literally get their hands dirty. Mud should be mixed by hand in a bowl with salt and rye seeds. This ointment should be allowed to stay on the hands for six minutes without being rinsed in order to loosen up the Virgo. You may also do this ritual on yourself and then shake hands with a Virgo. Of course your hands must be clean when you attempt this. The effects will be more subtle than direct application, but little by little, through this contact high, you are sure to alleviate the annoying Virgo symptoms.

There is one area where the Virgo can be downright down and dirty. They are the best gossips of the zodiac! They remember and repeat all the juicy and lurid details. To stop slanderous talk, make a solution of salt water and rye and soak a piece of paper with the name of the tattletale inscribed upon it. This will stop the evil talk.

THE LUSTY LIBRA

INGREDIENTS

passion fruit

Libra occupies the seventh astrological house of love and marriage. It is the sign of partnership, true love and soul mates. When the scales of Venus tip, the Libra dips into lust and longs to couple with everyone in sight. For they are in love with love more often than they are in love with their partners. Libras also love to share. I know a Libran man who loves his girlfriend, loves his best friend's wife and girlfriend, loves the waitress in the local cafe, and her sister. . . . The list goes on and needless to say, the maestro has slept with them all. He sees this as the ultimate act of sharing and continues to woo every beautiful chick, completely oblivious to the carnage he leaves in his wake. The only difference between the Libra and neighbor Scorpio, in their capacity for lust, is that the Scorpio calls it like it is: "a delicious deadly sin!" But the Libra will tell you: "it's Love!" Oh, the charming Libran definitely outdoes the Scorpion with carnal cravings, although they rarely match the intensity of Scorpio passion.

Speaking of passion, passion fruit is an excellent food for self-control and to curb sexual desire. I know it doesn't sound that way, but the fruit and flower actually have historical and magical lore associating them with fidelity and true love. The fruit is also said to help solve domestic problems and prevent lust from choking the heart. For when all is said and done the Libra needs a deep, constant, loving relationship to be fulfilled. Unfortunately the ruling planet manifests in its yang aspect and the hard-edged masculine drive easily succumbs to sexual shallowness when badly aspected. An out of balance Libran should eat passion fruit to calm and subdue the voracious appetite of Venus.

THE GREEN EYED MONSTER

INGREDIENTS
a string of dried red jalapeno peppers

It is said that when an angel falls, he falls lower than a man, for he becomes a demon. When a man falls, he falls lower than an animal, for animals do not murder for sport, although they may kill for food or survival. When an animal falls, they fall lower than plant life, for the rotting of dead flesh is more putrid than vegetation. When a plant falls, it becomes lower than a mineral or rock for it loses its substance and form.

When Scorpios fall, they fall lower than any other sign and

into the depths of the abyss. Contrary to popular belief, it is not Aries, but Scorpio who is potentially the most selfish of the signs. Scorpio rules death and regeneration, but when the Scorpio falls, he connects only with death and loses touch with rebirth. The ego, fearful of its own mortality, becomes blown out of proportion and spits and fights vehemently against ensuing death. The Scorpio at its lowest point is envious, vengeful, jealous and spiteful. After losing its wings, all it possesses is the stinging tail.

Ouch! It is the deadly sin of envy that plagues the Scorpio. There is a remedy for this dreadful curse. In the same way that garlic is carried to repel vampires, dried red peppers (or even red gemstones carved in this shape) can be worn, carried in the pocket, or hung within the home to ward off the envious feelings of another. Fresh red peppers can be eaten to purge envy or jealousy from the soul.

THE STINGING ARROW

INGREDIENTS

figs

"Do you swear to tell the truth, the whole truth and nothing but the truth, so help you God!?" Ah, the blunt truth-tellers of the zodiac, and the Sagittarian brings God into the equation as well. Dogmatism is their downfall and being deceit-free is their detriment. With all their infinite wisdom and walls of Ph.D.s, the Sagittarian never learned about the *little white lie*. They know it all, and they tell it like it is. How insensitive of the finer graceful details is their telescopic view. It allows them to ride roughshod over others, all in the name of Honesty. It's horseshit and it hurts!

The fig is a deceitful fruit. Some biblical commentaries state that it was a fig and not an apple that the Serpent used to tempt and seduce Eve. Do you think she would have taken a bite of anything if the Old Snake had told her up front about labor pains?! The fig is not only wise but crafty. The knowledge of good and evil can help the Sagittarian determine the right from the WRONG things to say. The fig is grounded and earthy. It can yank the foot out of the mouth and pull the posterior down from that presumptuous peremptory place in the sky. Count on this fruit to lead the archer back to the forest of infinite possibilities. For this is the exalted hunting ground of the Sag.

THE GREEDY GOAT

INGREDIENTS

your checkbook or credit card
assorted dried grains

Conjure up the image of the billygoat munching on everything in sight, including tin cans. At the same time one of his eyes is set on the greener grass across the fence. This image portrays the weakness of the sign of Capricorn. They can be greedy little goats, gobbling up whatever is in reach. Saturn makes the spirit tough, austere and enduring. But an overdose of heavy Saturn can kill off generosity of the spirit, opening the door to the deadly sin of avarice.

New York City is a goat and perfectly illustrates the power of Capricornian greed. Just take a look at the real estate market in Manhattan if you want to witness true avarice. In the month of Capricorn, in 2002, the famous Coliseum bookstore went out of business because their rent was raised 300%. Even though the majority of downtown spaces were dropping in value after September 11, 2001, landlords with deregulated apartments continued to play hardball with greedy bases full. Despite the 4.2 million dollars (1.2 million was donated by Bette Midler, a philanthropic Sag) raised to save the downtown community gardens, too many were lost. Perhaps the most poignant of these losses was the *Esperanza* garden. *Esperanza* means hope, and the fact that this *hope* (along with strong political action and protest) was conquered by avarice is more than just a symbolic defeat. The city-owned public land was sold to one of the most unethical and greedy developers for next to nothing. Neighborhood children lost their little bit of green, and instead of following regulations and creating low- and middle-income housing, the developer built luxury apartments. The buildings themselves are anything but luxurious. They are boney, boring, grim and bleak Capricornian-style structures.

The only thing that is luxury is the price!

There are two very good remedies for overcoming greed. If your problem is greediness for money, the best remedy is to give money to a charitable cause. This will give you karmic brownie points and invoke the spirit of generosity into your soul. It is even effective to give charity on someone else's behalf. Send a donation to your favorite charity in the name of a certain greedy person. Also let this person know that a donation has been made on his or her behalf. The effects are subtle but the undercurrent runs deep. The second method is used when something other than money is being coveted. Capricorns are notorious for coveting power, status, property and position (and on rare occasions, the neighbors wife). In such cases, a fistful of mixed dried grains must be tossed over the left shoulder. Grains are sacred to Ops, the wife of Saturn. She is the goddess of plenty who magically refills the cornucopia of life. Spilling her sacred grains will help you to let go of coveting and trust that your own life will be full of the bounty of Ops, enough so that you will gratefully share what you have with others. Grains can also be tossed from the inside of a greedy establishment to draw wealth out. Go inside, open a window and toss out a handful of grains to turn the karmic dollar around.

EMOTIONAL ARCTIC ZONE

INGREDIENTS

brazil nuts

Aquarians suffer from emotional detachment. The great humanitarian has a severe price to pay when the love of freedom makes the heart grow cold. On a personal level, they may remain aloof to avoid relationships. Fear of intimacy plagues this sign. On a more global level, Aquarians believe in the good of all mankind above the well-being of the individual human life. When badly aspected, Aquarian energy will produce suicide bombers willing to give up their lives and the lives of innocent others in exchange for ideals and principles. The greatest sages teach that when one life ceases to become precious or meaningful, then all life becomes worthless.

The best example of an Aquarian gone awry is the mad scientist who used humans for experimentation; Josef Mengele, known as the Angel of Death in the Nazi concentration camps, had Mars in Aquarius. Mengele had the placement in 00 or 01 degrees. The early degrees created a young Mars with infantile rage coupled with a naive Aquarian influence lending group idealistic support to the Doctor's deadly designs. Pluto in Gemini squaring the Sun and Mercury explains his obsession with experimentation on twins. Mengele, by the way, had the sun in Pisces; the sign of suffering. With the strong Mars placement creating a cold, calculating, sadistic and purely scientific drive, Mengele managed to inflict enormous suffering.

The Waterbearer often travels in cold murky waters. Aquarius needs to warm up to the one-on-one joys of relating spirit-to-spirit. Only then can the sign deal with the group as a whole. Brazil nuts are closely connected to the Waterbearer. The fat nut is full of love and will help the Aquarian to connect one-on-one. Heart-to-heart. The outer skin of the brazil nut should be removed. The heart of the nut should be eaten or pulverized and added to very hot bathwater. This should be done whenever an Aquarian finds himself losing touch on a personal level.

THE LAZY FISH

INGREDIENTS

loofah sponge
seaweed scrub or dead sea salts

Sloth is the weakness of the sign of Pisces. It enters through the feet and causes the rest of the body to move at a snail's pace. The sluggish lazy Pisces is ruled by Neptune, the dreamer, and is therefore more vulnerable to idleness than any other sign. The tides of Neptune's ocean waters cause the fish to drift aimlessly about.

Here is a simple spell to school the fish away from indolence. You will need a loofah sponge and a seaweed scrub. You can also use dead sea salts. Take a hot bath and scrub the body down with the loofah using the seaweed scrub or dead sea salts. Begin with the feet and work your way up the body. Make sure you rotate the loofah in a clockwise direction, moving always in the direction of the heart. This ritual will invigorate the body and is believed to give zeal to the soul. These three ingredients of the sea are believed to cleanse and lend energy to the flesh and spirit.

Pisces will notice best results when performing this bath on a new moon. You may also take a ritual foot bath to help you get up on your feet and take action. Other signs may also use this bath on new moons to combat laziness, or for optimum effects, perform it on the new moon in Pisces (February 18 or 19) or when the sun is in the sign of Pisces (February 18–March 20).

ADDICTION: THE 4 TYPES

The following is useful information to help create rituals to combat addiction. The twelve zodiac signs are broken down into four elements: Earth, Air, Fire and Water. The earth signs are Taurus, Virgo, and Capricorn. The air signs are Gemini, Libra, and Aquarius. The fire signs are Aries, Leo, and Sagittarius. The water signs are Cancer, Scorpio, and Pisces. Your sun sign or ascendant will determine the element of addiction you are most susceptible to.

Weaknesses in Earth signs lead to eating disorders, heroin use (because it comes from the poppy plant), gambling and any kind of repetitive physical abuse to the body.

Smoking is an air addiction but also relates to the elements of fire (heat) and earth (tobacco plants). The air signs are also susceptible to negative thinking patterns.

An imbalance of fire energy inflames the passions. Pyromania, temper tantrums, physical abuse directed toward others and sexual addiction fall under this element.

Water addictions include alcoholism, abuse of hallucinogenic drugs and emotional dependency.

Vanilla bean or extract, ginger root and brick dust are the ingredients of a traditional and very powerful witch's brew to combat addiction. A fourth ingredient should be added to

gear the potion toward the element of addiction you are trying to overcome.

Earth—salt
Air—sage
Fire—black pepper
Water—coconut

These four are often used for purification, cleansing and
control. To prepare this potion, mix the original three ingredients into a small jar. Add the fourth elemental ingredient. Seal
the jar with the wax drippings of a brown candle (earth),
white candle (air), red candle (fire), or blue candle (water). A
wax seal is used by witches for empowerment. Shake this bottle as much as possible to give you strength in overcoming your
addiction. For optimum success, use the witch's addiction bottle along with other forms of help to combat your problem.

SPECIALITY ⊕F +HE H⊕USE

Each sign is blessed with a special quality. These spells are designed to share the best of each sign with all.

MY FAVORITE MARTIAN

INGREDIENTS
red, black, and white ground pepper

Aries excels in leadership. Other signs can learn how to take charge from the Ram. The fearless Aries is not afraid to be on the frontlines. You will not find cowards or traitors among this sign. Red, black, and white pepper are the most treasured spices of the warrior god, Mars. Use them to invoke his strength or win his favor. Sprinkle the tri-colored peppers on foods eaten on a Tuesday during sunlight hours.

The Aries can season in all seasons to bring forth the positive qualities of Mars and dispel meekness. Other signs may use on Tuesdays when the sun is in Aries (March 21–April 19) to muster up the mastering spirit.

THE SENSUAL BULL

INGREDIENTS

guava or guava jelly

The sensual Taurus can teach us all a thing or two about how to live in the present and enjoy each and every moment of life. *Carpe diem* is definitely a Taurus motto. The bull holds on to each precious moment and cherishes it without distraction. The Taurus sinks his teeth into all of life. The admirable ability to feel pleasure is the greatest blessing of this sign.

The myth of Aphrodite and Adonis is linked to Taurus. Adonis was killed by a wild boar and sent to the underworld. When Aphrodite was separated from Adonis, she mourned and the earth became barren and cold; there was no love between men and women. When Adonis returned to her, the earth blossomed once again. The god and goddess took pleasure in each other and granted this joy to men and women. The month of Taurus (April 21–June 20) is the time of reunion for Adonis and Aphrodite. Those born at this time have their sun in opposition to Scorpio. This keen awareness of death and separation at the other end compels them to stubbornly hold on to both the spiritual and the material pleasures of this world.

The guava fruit is rich and juicy and represents the fertile womb of the goddess swimming with the seed of the god. It is a fruit of pleasure and can be eaten to induce and prolong gratification. Eat guava to open up your capacity for joy. The most sacred day to eat the fruit is on May first. This is Beltane, one of the four greater Sabbats of the witches. When eaten on this day, not only will you begin to recognize the pleasures great and small that you already possess—the god and goddess will bless you with tenfold more!

THE WONDERFUL WIT

INGREDIENTS

speckled beans
mercury thermometer

Geminis are the wittiest sign of the zodiac. They are clever and quick and always have a comeback. They are also the branch of the zodiac tribe that was gifted with the sacred art of channeling and communication. Since this is the sign of the twins, there are two spells. The first is to improve your sense of humor, or find it if you have lost it. To tickle your funny bone, place a large bowl of dried speckled or split beans in front of you. Grab handfuls of the beans and toss them above your head while laughing out loud. This releases tiny spirits of humor. The speckled and split beans are said to be the ones who carried humor into the world. Hermes sent them to earth to teach humanity how to laugh and be clever.

You can also eat speckled beans on Wednesdays and carry them in your pocket to sharpen your wag.

The second spell is used to receive information and intelligence. Obtain a mercury thermometer and place it under your tongue. Make a mental inquiry about some information you wish to obtain. This question may concern worldly or otherworldly matters. Remove the thermometer after you have clearly formed your question and shake it. Hold it between your palms for three minutes. Repeat every Wednesday until relevant information comes into your mind or hands. Gemini is ruled by Mercury and liquid mercury is the most sacred element of his work. To **safely** connect with the element will give you the strongest link with this god of intelligence.

THERE'S NO PLACE LIKE HOME

INGREDIENTS

dried crab claw shell
half a coconut husk
powdered egg shell
earl grey (bergamot) tea
beer
mistletoe

21Aug01: Rudely awakened at six A.M. by the boom, bang and blast of the construction behind my building. A bad night's sleep as I had been tossing and turning most of the night debating whether or not to sign my new lease with the $500 monthly rent increase. I've got to write some spells today, but the sounds are intolerable. I contemplate performing a spell to kill the workmen and the landlord. A coffee shop on a quieter street seems like a better option. (Takes a lot less energy and is more in line with my overall plan for the day.) With my notebook in tow, off I go.

I catch a glimpse of the headline on today's paper. EVICTION MARSHAL SLAIN IN B'KLYN. A woman threw the marshal over a second-floor railing, beat him with an aluminum stick, doused him with gasoline and set him on fire. I felt an uncensored rush of glee surge through my body. Pure unadulterated joy. Under normal circumstances, I would probably have felt mortified. But today was a bad day; I had been driven from my home. I took pleasure in the fact that some crazy woman in Crown Heights was able to freely express her rage—to fully defend her home. So what if she owed $14,000 in back rent!? Was that any reason to evict her?!

I knew first-hand how over-inflated New York rents were. On August twenty-first, the moon was squaring Jupiter in Cancer and Jupiter was conjoined in the north node—signifying overblown emotional, financial, and karmic issues concerning Cancerian territory: the home. WOW! The lady in Crown Heights and I were pretty much on the same emotional wavelength. We just made different choices on how to act. But she got me thinking about the specialty of the sign of Cancer.

The strongest magic associated with the sign is the protection of the home. The crab is fierce in guarding his home—so fierce that his home is actually carried on his back. The crab never lets go of his home, it is part of his very flesh and being. It covers, shelters, and protects him. You can not force a crab out of his shell. If threatened, he will withdraw and hide within or he will attack and claw to defend his territory. The sign of Cancer is ruled by the moon and is therefore capable of the fullest emotional range. I found myself empathizing with the awesome anger this woman must have felt at losing her home. We live in an age where real estate is bought and sold as commodity. Housing and shelter have become secondary. Property no longer serves as a means to put a roof over someone's head. Unfortunately, this spell is too late for the eviction marshal and the lady in Brooklyn. He is now with God and she will probably no longer have to worry about affordable housing or back rent, as she now has a prison cell of her own. This spell is offered up for the law-abiding citizens that remain among us. Please use it before you find yourself setting marshals, landlords, tenants, neighbors or construction workers on fire.

The spell can be used by any sign at any time of the year as long as it is performed in the home. The home is always the space where the sign of Cancer dwells. A talisman can be made of a dried crab claw shell, half a coconut husk and powdered egg shell. Place the coconut husk behind the door of your dwelling as if it were a bowl. Place the crab claw shell in it and sprinkle powered eggshell over the claw. To make powdered eggshell you must save an eggshell from an egg you have used. Wash it and let it dry. Then powder the eggshell using a coffee grinder. The crab claw is a perfect magical symbol to cover, protect and shelter the home. Coconut is used for blessing and purification. Eggshell catches negativity and neutralizes it. All ingredients are owned by the sign of Cancer and when combined they create a sense of well-being and peace. Prepare this talisman whenever you feel threatened by anything concerning your home and keep it out until the situation has subsided. Renew when necessary.

11Sep01: Awakened at nine by a loud bang which shook the whole house. I had been up till 6 A.M. writing. I stared up at my roof. It was still there. I went back to sleep. Hours later I found out over the phone about the WTC attack. I decided to stay inside when I saw that my street had been blocked off to all traffic and was being used by emergency vehicles as a loading zone for ground zero. Calls were coming in all day with offers to escape to Connecticut, New Jersey, Florida, Buenos Aires, and Berlin. Connecticut was the only realistic option as Grand Central Terminal was still open and operating. But every bone in my body just wanted to stay put and defend my home on the Lower East Side and my homeland in New York City.

On September eleventh, the moon was void-of-course in Cancer. Four planes were taken off course and came crashing into our consciousness like the four apocalyptic horsemen, waking us up to an ominous time. The United States of America has its sun in Cancer. When a Sun/Moon conjunction occurs, solar energy (fire) overpowers the nurturing lunar principle. The moon in Cancer was also in opposition to Mars, a nasty configuration which can cause death through violence, war, or fires. The opposition can also bring conflict over money and property. New York City is a Capricorn and therefore had a Sun/Moon opposition and Mars/Sun conjunction. These aspects bring conflict and aggression. Saturn was also opposing Pluto, an aspect that was present at the onset of both the First and Second World Wars.

It was a bad day and I clung to the preciousness of my home. I had a cup of bergamot tea, which is said to guard against sudden attacks (again, perhaps this magic was a bit late, but in those hours and days following, we had no idea what was coming next). Later on I had a beer. Beer contains hops or Flores de Cerveza. Ruled by Mars, this plant is best for healing in wartime or war zones. In the liquid form of beer, hops also has strong associations with the moon and can help calm the emotions. I want to stress that I drank only ONE beer. In times of high alert it is unwise to deaden the senses with too much alcohol or drugs. The events of this tragic day forced me to think deeply about this spell. Protecting one's own home is not enough. The homeland must be protected as well. I spread a map of New York City upon my altar and sprinkled the borders with loose bergamot tea. Using cotton swabs, I anointed the ground zero area with beer. If you would like to lend magical energy to the security of your homeland, obtain a map of the city, state, country that you wish to protect. Surround its borders with loose bergamot tea and anoint sensitive spots with beer.

11Oct01: One month later and still this spell did not seem complete. It needed a chant. I had been up all night searching through obscure books of shadows, looking for just the right litany to the Moon Goddess. I came to the conclusion, at four A.M., that there is a reason for their obscurity. Nothing in these books seemed to hold the weight or power or exact message that I was looking for. I drifted off to sleep. I was awakened at nine A.M. by an angelic voice singing into my answering machine:

> *"Casta Diva che inargenti*
> *Queste sacre antiche piante*
> *A noi volgi il bel sembiante*
> *Senza nube e senza vel!"*

Some words followed: "Wake up Bruja Diva. We've got tickets for Norma. Esta Noche. It's opening night. Call me back after your latte!" It was a message from my wonderful friend Renata. She is a soprano and has amazing connections at the Met. Needless to say, I was quite excited to be invited to the opera that night, but I was even more excited that Renata had delivered the missing piece of the puzzle for which I searched. This discovery only reaffirmed my belief in my own work. Magic and the Goddess dance right in front of our eyes, never hidden from those who truly seek.

In all my years as a witch and high priestess, I have had the opportunity to read dozens of books of shadows with litanies to the Goddess. And in all the secret books I was privy to, not one can compare with the most beautiful litany to the Goddess I have ever heard, a litany that is quite public and not at all hidden. I am referring to the "Casta Diva," the prayer to the Chaste Moon Goddess in Bellini's opera *Norma*. Norma is a Druid priestess. In the "Casta Diva" Norma performs the sacred rite of cutting mistletoe with a sickle under the light of the full moon. This is her prayer:

> *Chaste Goddess, who bathes in silver light*
> *these ancient, hallow trees,*
> *turn thy fair face upon us,*
> *unveiled and unclouded!*
> *Temper, O Goddess,*
> *temper thou the burning hearts,*
> *the excessive zeal,*
> *the excessive zeal of thy people.*
> *Enfold the earth, ah, in peace,*
> *enfold the earth in that sweet peace*
> *which through thee reigns in heaven,*
> *which reigns in heaven.*

Here is what was missing. A prayer to temper the excessive zeal of the woman in Brooklyn. The excessive zeal of the terrorists. The excessive zeal of angry Americans now attacking innocent Arab-Americans. A prayer to the Moon Goddess in her state of fullness, asking her to envelop our home, the earth, in peace.

It was a bad night at the opera but I showed up dressed to the nines for the hometown. It was my first real night out in over a month. Very eerie to be searched with a metal detector and have your bag checked at the Metropolitan Opera. Before 9/11 I would have cheered for the Druids, but that night the Druid priest looked surreally like Osama bin Laden. And when they sang the lines about clipping the wings of Rome's great eagle, well, I just about lost it. Norma seemed way too close to home. Renata calmed me down by reminding me that it took 500 years to overthrow the Roman Empire. "Never happen in our lifetimes," she assured me. With Renata's hand resting on my knee, I began to think that all might once again be right with the world. And THEN—Jane Eaglen sang the "Casta Diva" off key. I was a basketcase. Convinced it was a sign of bad magic, overcome with excessive zeal, I ran home to watch my 1978 videotape of Norma, with Montserrat Caballé singing the "Casta Diva." Caballé is the most powerful priestess I have ever seen. The sickle in her hand yields incredible power. And the voice—there are no words—only ears for the voice.[10]

To invoke peace upon the earth, sing, chant, or listen to the "Casta Diva" under a full moon while waving a branch of freshly-cut mistletoe. Place this mistletoe over the door of

---

[10]Available through the Bel Canto Society. I recommend using this video or CD in your ritual.

your home to bring personal peace and protection to your house and family. This ritual is highly effective for relieving stress and worry and creating a peaceful yet alert state of being. The light of the full moon summons watchfulness and revelations or the shedding of light upon things. The mistletoe weeds out excessive worry or zeal. Perform this ritual on any full moon[11] to invoke peace for the homeland and for your own personal household.

THE SHINING STAR

INGREDIENTS

golden apple
honeycomb

The noble lion knows how to shine. This cat possesses incredible will power and self-esteem. The Leo loves to take center stage and knows that shyness is not a virtue. Gregarious, entertaining, social and warmhearted, this solar-powered sign can teach us all how to roar. The leonine ego is enormous. There is plenty to go around.

Use this Leo spell to overcome shyness, stage fright, or lack of self-confidence or self-love. Use it to create a charismatic aura before you put yourself out front. On a Sunday, take a golden apple and cut it in half horizontally. You should see a five-pointed star in the center of both halves. Drizzle honey from a honeycomb into the open halves, then match the halves

---

[11]Every full moon, regardless of what sign it is in, holds the vibration of the sign of Cancer.

up and hold the apple together in one piece. Eat this apple to instill the golden elixir of the sun into your inner core.

Golden apples represent the sun conjoined with Venus. They summon self-love, self-confidence, recognition and fame. Honey drawn from a natural honeycomb is sacred to the sun and represents an inner connection with the Divine. This creates inner beauty that shines outward like the radiant rays of the sun.

SPELL TO CLEAN UP A MESS

INGREDIENTS

flour
salt
lemon
baking soda

We all know that cleanliness is next to god/dessliness, but the Virgo masters this to perfection. Discriminating, hygienic, analytical—they really can clean up any situation. So, if you have created some kind of mess in your life, this is the spell for you. Doesn't matter if we are talking about a filthy house, disheveled appearance, messed-up relationship, a dirty mind or habit—Virgo magic can scrub it all clean. This spell will not manifest a housekeeper out of thin air or turn mice into tailors to design you new clothes. It will not pay for your couple's counseling or your 1900LiveSexTalk bill. It will give you the energy and organization to begin tidying up these affairs.

Prepare a bath with a pinch of flour, three cups of salt,

lemon juice, lemon peel, and a teaspoonful of baking soda. Hey, don't throw that leftover baking soda away. Place it in your stinky fridge to absorb the foul odors. Virgo is practical and frugal. Waste not, want not. Soak in this bath for a minimum of ten minutes. All the ingredients are sacred to Virgo and are used for purging and purification. Dry off and get dressed. Immediately take some small detailed action to remedy your situation. You are not going to solve it all or clean it all up in that moment. But you can make a dent. This is how Virgo energy operates. It allows us to focus on one small task at a time and not get discouraged by the big overwhelming picture.

KARMIC SCALES

INGREDIENTS

a red feather

Yes, yes, Libra is the sign of lovers but its greater gift is that it has been assigned the responsibility for the scales of justice. It stands to reason that it is the only sign not depicted by human or animal representation. The scales of the goddess Ma'at were chosen to symbolize Libra. She rules the karmic balance of the world. Her symbol is the red feather. She weighs the souls of both the dead and the living and was the most powerful goddess in ancient Egypt.

Invoking justice or calling down karma is a serious business but we can count on Libra, more than any other sign, to be fair. You can not use this spell to exact revenge. Do not attempt to control the outcome, leave that in the hands of Ma'at.

Write down the matter or deed that calls for a just decision. Include the names of all parties seeking justice as well as the offenders. Ma'at was coupled with Thoth, the god of writing. It is in the tradition of Thoth that cases are argued. Fold the paper as small as you can. Place it in the center of the inside of the feather. Rock the paper back and forth within the cradle of the feather. Ask Ma'at for justice. Place the feather on an altar surrounded by any documents connected with the case or issue. Do not remove until justice has been served.

TOWER MAGIC

INGREDIENTS

sixteen eggs

Alongside the scorpion, the snake and eagle (also phoenix) are also closely linked to the sign of Scorpio. The specialty of Scorpio is its ability to recycle, revive, and reinvent itself. The sign rules death and rebirth. The energies of this solar month and this solar sign can teach us many things about moving on. . . .

In mid-September of 2000 I was fired from my job of nearly twenty years. I, along with other employees, was not only let go, but "banished," badmouthed, and blamed for the shortcomings of the business. This blow came after years of working for peanuts while holding out for the dangling carrot of becoming a partner. Meanwhile, the business flourished under my spell. My books brought in hoards of clients and the shop always got a mention in the numerous national radio, television, and newsprint interviews I gave. I certainly did my part. Needless to say, I was stunned and heartbroken at being betrayed by supposed "sisters of the craft," friends, women I had trusted and worked hard for. In the month that followed I also felt stinging rage and bitterness which led me to the most archetypal and notorious feeling that Scorpio is traditionally associated with: **REVENGE!**

Before I knew it, Samhain (Halloween) or the Witches' New Year had arrived. I knew it was time for some serious magic. That night I had a dream in which one of my old familiars appeared. His name was Angel and he was a beautiful Burmese Python. Angel's death had actually coincided with my first days of working in this occult shop. In the dream he looked quite the same except for the addition of a pair of glorious wings. Angel wrapped these wings around my body and together we shed a skin. I woke up feeling refreshed, released, and renewed. The anger, the bitterness, the sorrow and pain all seemed to float away on that morning after Angel and I shed our skins.[12] The snake also spoke some words to me on the astral. Whhissspered them in my ear.

"Take sixteen eggs," he said. "Symbols of rebirth. Symbols of change. Symbols of the time of Scorpio."

"Why sixteen?" I asked.

"The number of the Tower card in the Tarot. Did your world not come crashing down? Fear not. It is only the walls of your prison disintegrating. You are now free. Take these eggs and crack open the shells. Transform the shapeless embryos within them as you would transform yourself. Make them a

---

[12]Also, I should not neglect to mention the month and a half of intense psychotherapy that preceded the dream.

thing of beauty. This ritual will reinforce your release and renewal. Beautiful phoenix—rise up from these ashes."

Thus spoke the serpent.

I woke up that morning rather perplexed and extremely hungry. Before I knew it, I was cracking open a couple of eggs and staring at the shapeless blobs in the bowl. I thought of the endless days of boredom I had spent in that shop, going nowhere. I took a deep breath and inhaled the coffee brewing. It was a new day and it belonged to me. I threw a pinch of salt and a dollop of milk into the eggs for purification and nurturing. I energetically beat them to a froth. For the first time in over a month, I felt inspired. Over a hot flame I made those shapeless eggs rise up into a perfect fluffy **omelet.** I devoured it and then sat down to spend the day working on my long-neglected novel. How wonderfully joyous. On the second morning I made eggs **sunny side up.** It made me smile just to know that my days would never ever begin again in that dingy, dusty old shop. I spent the morning harvesting lavender in my garden. Never again would I have to greet the day in such bad company. Day three the eggs were **over easy.** That's when I got the phone call from my friend Bert. He had been bugging me (along with countless others) to build a Web site. On day three, I said yes to Bert. He is the great-great-grandson of the famous Yiddish writer Shalom Aleichem and built the official Web site for Shalom. I liked the decision I made on that day. It felt great to be in such company. After years of agonizing over the Web site issue, it happened almost overnight on the third day. On the fourth morning I made **french toast**[13] with

---

[13]See "Buttering Up the Gods," the french toast money spell in *Easy Enchantments.* (St. Martins Press 1999)

my eggs and the money started to roll in over the phone. Lots of clients called for private consultations. Cool! I made some **hard boiled** on the fifth day and some **soft boiled** on the sixth day to try and gain insight on how to organize my time. The freelance artist must learn when to be flexible and when to be fixed. On day seven I **poached** my eggs. I also pocketed some extra money after being able to pay my bills. It was the first time since I lost my job that I'd been able to do that. I also met a few people on the street that day who complained to me about the serious state of decline the shop had fallen into. You might think that information fell like fresh game upon my ears, but my new reality made me feel like a trespasser in a distant land I wanted no part of. On the eighth day I **scrambled** the eggs. Perhaps this was a mistake, but one can always learn from mistakes. On that day, my ex-boss's crazy mother left me a very disturbing voice mail. These messages continued periodically for over a year. Even though I had gracefully and successfully moved on, they seemed to be stuck in the past. The most recent voice mail to date was received in October of 2001. I was accused of sending her an anthrax-laced letter and was warned that the FBI would be investigating the matter. Yes, of course it (along with all the previous messages) provoked a momentary mental scrambling. I wondered if I should call my lawyer. I considered calling back to defend my honor, sanity, dignity, and decency as an American citizen and citizen of the world. I would never send an anonymous letter with seemingly sinister contents. It's not my style. If I have something to say, good or bad, I usually choose to say it right out loud, **in bold print,** for thousands of people to read, with my name attached to it. I would also never, ever choose a cowardly action such as taking advantage of a national crisis and panic to terrorize a personal or political enemy. Again, it's not my style. And scrambled eggs or not, I also realized it is not my style to get scrambled up with people who are beyond reason, who hunger for, and feed off, anger and dissension. I do not respond. I do not engage. Each voice mail rolls off my back like a dead skin I have shed, remaining in the ashes I have risen above. Scorpio is the eighth sign of the zodiac.

I recommend the Eight Day Egg Spell (two eggs a day) when serious transformation and renewal are needed. The spell can be worked by Scorpios at any time of the year. Other signs are advised to use it between October 21–November 20.

SPELL FOR ADVENTURE

INGREDIENTS

duck or goose

Sagittarians are the explorers, adventures, and travelers of the zodiac. They know how to move in mind, body, and spirit. Use this spell to invoke adventure or more travel into your life. The duck is the king of fowl. He can travel through the air and flies in migratory patterns. He can swim on the water and dive under it. He can walk on land. (The goose can not dive under the water which is why he is only a prince.) Eating duck can invoke more travel and adventure into your life. If you are a vegetarian, you should seek out duck or geese, listen to their sounds and try to mimic them as you visualize your travel plans. Duck dances were very popular among the rituals of several Native American tribes. The sound *quack quack* was made while imitating the walk of a duck. Use the energy of the duck to enhance movement and growth in your life, whether material, mental, emotional, or spiritual.

THE JACK BENNY SPELL

INGREDIENTS
apple cider vinegar

Capricorn knows how to age gracefully. This is due to the innate understanding and connection with Saturn possessed by the sign. Use Capricorn magic to be at peace with your age. The spell is designed for women, but men may find it useful as well. I know many women who begin to lie about their age when they reach twenty-nine. Interesting, because this is the year of the Saturn return. The planet will weigh heavily on you if you have not accepted responsibility and taken power over your life in the twenty-ninth year. By forty, it's all over. The fibbing escalates and the Jack Benny syndrome kicks in for good.

Capricorn rules the tenth house, which is the arena of the world. Traditionally the forties, fifties, and sixties are the pinnacle-of-power years for public leaders, politicians, and those who exert global influence. Those who lie about their age deny themselves the power that age brings. It may keep them immature, but it will not make them younger. When accepted and incorporated correctly and fully, Saturn brings wisdom and influence. When denied, the planet offers restriction and sorrow. Deny your true age and you deny your power and profundity. You confine yourself to a tight box you have long ago outgrown. The best example of this is a bad face-lift with skin pulled so tight it draws attention to, instead of masking, the austerity of Saturn. The face is eerily devoid of the deep dissipation that defines and tells the story of a life well lived. The only hint of insight left stares out from the experience-filled eyes trapped in their cage of denial. I am not giving a thumbs-down to body beautification or the pursuit of youthful looks, I am simply saying that acceptance works wonders for the aging process. Get yourself on the right side of Saturn and you will feel good no matter how you choose to deal with that old and inevitable devil known as gravity. The worst thing about aging is that it brings us closer to death. The reality, however, is that death can come calling no matter how old you are. Enjoy living your age and reap the benefits of it.

Apple cider vinegar is a very special ingredient because it is sacred to the Triple Goddess. It incorporates all three of her aspects: Maiden, Mother, and Crone. In astrological terms, it would be a magical conjunction of Venus and Saturn, therefore invoking the beauty of any age. With liberation and acceptance the Maiden and Mother flow back into the Crone. Apple cider vinegar helps to keep this circle of energy rotating. It clears the way for youthfulness, innocence, sensuality, and sexuality to flow through an older wiser person. Drink a tablespoon of apple cider vinegar or add a cupful to the bathwater on your birthday, the New Year, or any Saturday that you feel depressed or in denial about your age.

FRIENDSHIP AND FREEDOM SPELLS

INGREDIENTS

FRIENDSHIP:

rosebuds

vanilla bean

cinnamon

spearmint

FREEDOM:

coconut

cinnamon

lemon

bay

Aquarius rules the eleventh house of friendship and freedom. The bonds formed through the eleventh house are deeper than the surface social activity generated from the fifth house. The ego and the sex drive derive their fulfillment from the fifth house whereas the eleventh house seeks to provide freedom and liberty for the individual.

Aquarius can teach us how to align ourselves with group energy. The friendship spell should be used to draw a group of people that you feel spiritually in tune with. It is a great recipe to use when you feel out of touch and lonely or know that you are mixed in with bad and superficial company. Crush a handful of rosebuds and dried spearmint leaves. Grind a vanilla bean. Place contents into a bowl. Add cinnamon powder. This mixture can be added to the bathwater or carried in a pouch in the pocket. It is a great blend to place out in the open or sprinkle around a room before a special event or board meeting. Use it whenever you wish for unity, understanding and connection between people.

Rose is the flower most often used to attract friendship. Vanilla opens channels for love. Combined with spearmint, the focus shifts from physical (sexual) to mental and emotional love. Cinnamon helps with bonding, connection, and communication.

To create more freedom and liberty in your personal life prepare a mixture of dried coconut flakes, cinnamon powder, dried lemon peel, and crushed bay leaves. Sprinkle this mixture on the floor and walk across it. These ingredients are sacred to the god Legba, who opens the crossroads and removes obstacles from the path. This mixture can also be used to get out of jail. Repeat every Monday until your goal is achieved.

PSYCHIC POWER SPELL

INGREDIENTS

cinnamon
coriander
cardamom
licorice
sage

Pisces is the mystic of the zodiac. Neptune's blessing of fertile imagery places the most talented artists and psychics among this sign. The imagination or psychic senses can be stimulated by use of this traditional piscean witches' brew. Make a tea with small amounts of cinnamon stick, coriander, cardamom, licorice, and sage. Drink by the light of the moon or near the sea to heighten your creative or intuitive powers. You may also use these ingredients on the full moon for a ritual bath. Coriander and cardamom distract the guardians of the gates allowing entrance to the subconscious or creative mind. Sage and cinnamon help us reach states of meditation and trance. Licorice wands are used to channel divine energy. They hold a very strong yin vibration which creates sensitivity and receptiveness to the unseen worlds.

Note: Pregnant women and anyone with allergies to these ingredients should not drink or use near the skin. You may however place dried ingredients in a satchel and carry or place on the altar.

FINAL SPECIALTY SPELL

INGREDIENTS

cinnamon
bay leaves

If you have a positive attribute you want to enhance, (one that I haven't chosen) here is a spell to lend more power to your own personal specialty. Carve your name and your quality into your astral candle. Rub the candle with cinnamon powder and surround it with crushed bay leaves. Burn to completion.

Cinnamon and bay can be used to accentuate positive qualities and they always bring success. Here is a list of the astral colors.

Aries—red
Taurus—green
Gemini—Lavender
Cancer—silver or white
Leo—yellow or gold
Virgo—pink
Libra—red or yellow
Scorpio—purple
Sagittarius—orange
Capricorn—brown or dark red
Aquarius—light blue
Pisces—light green

AF✝ERW⊕RD

29Jan02: I have just finished my first gnocchi[14] night of the year. I must say that I was somewhat dubious about this gnocchi money spell. Money magic from Argentina seems pretty risky in light of the recent economic disasters to have befallen that country. We ate the gnocchi with a bolognese sauce. It was quite delicious. Meat sauce is very grounding and I have to say that I felt very centered and financially secure. But that is because this book is finished and I already know that a check from my publisher will be in the mail! But once the check arrives, most of it will go to pay the bills. The rest will be for taxes. By the second helping of bolognese I had sunk into a deep depression. I desperately need a vacation, but it's not in the budget.

"We were at the edge of the abyss. Now we have taken a step forward" kept running through my mind. The famous

---

[14]see Gnocchi Money Spell

faux pas of Argentine President Carlos Saúl Menem. I always think of Argentina when I think things can't get any worse. Because they can and the Argentines will attest to that.

But tonight things got a whole lot better. Before I had even removed the dollar from under my gnocchi plate I was offered a discount airline ticket and an apartment in Venice. Wow! Italy! I was thinking maybe I could afford trainfare to Baltimore. As far as I'm concerned, the Argentine gnocchi spell works like a charm. It's already saved me a lot of cash (my friends paid for the fabulous dinner) and made a holiday dream come true. I can't wait to do it again next month. O, hmm, well, next month doesn't have a twenty-ninth day this year. That's OK. I'll be in Italy. Plenty of fountains to throw coins in with my toes.[15]

I have one final word to say to you about magic. It works a lot like the Ronco Showtime Rotisserie Oven is supposed to work. Have you ever seen the infomercial? Every time Ron Popeil puts something in the oven and says, "SET IT—," that big excited studio audience completes the phrase with "AND FORGET IT!" Well, my friend Madeleine bought the Ronco and that's not really true. Madeleine got a really cool package that came with the BBQ gloves, utensils, all the different cooking baskets and a video tape. The first thing Ron tells you on that video is that you can't really "FORGET IT." You've got to pay attention. Madeleine's chicken even caught fire once because she forgot to follow some of Ron's cooking instructions. Now, don't get me wrong, I believe the Ronco is a wonderous thing as long as you keep a close watch. Magic,

---

[15]see Step into Money Spell

however, is completely the opposite. Once you "SET IT," you really do need to "FORGET IT" and let it go! To "set" a spell means to activate it. To activate it means to complete it. Once you have completed a spell, you need to forget about it. If you hold on to the magic and fret about it, it will never work. Think of the spell as a homing pigeon with a very important message tied to its feet. Throw it out with as much energy as you can summon and let it fly. Then go on about your business. The magic "pigeon" knows his way back. Don't yank his chain while he's on his delivery route. OK. I guess you've got that.

Good luck and good magic.

Blessed be

Lexa Roséan